Kauai Travel and Adventure Guide

The Ultimate Shortcut to Thrills, Beauty, and Culture, and Authentic Experiences

Ocean Breeze Adventures

Dedication

To my wife, who always has my back and loves to go on crazy adventures with me.

Contents

Praise for Ocean Breeze Adventures

KAUAI-As someone who only visited **Kauai** as a child and is now actively planning to bring my own small kids for a visit, this book provided far more insight into this unique island than I anticipated. It goes miles beyond a traditional guide book with top restaurant reviews and taxi info (even though it has that too). I was thrilled to get a history lesson, a deep dive into the history and learn about all the varied areas of this island. Well worth it for anyone seriously planning a trip!

-Amazon Reviewer

OAHU- Before our romantic anniversary trip to Hawaii, I picked up this eBook, and it was the perfect companion for our adventure. The book's practical advice and insider tips made our trip stress-free and memorable. We followed the recommendation to hike Diamond Head at sunrise, and the panoramic views were nothing short of breathtaking—definitely worth the early wake-up call. One of my favorite moments was ziplining at Kualoa Ranch; the thrill of soaring over Jurassic Valley was something we'll never forget.

The guide's suggestions for local eateries led us to some hidden gems, including a food truck serving the most delicious poke bowls. We also made time for a healing lomi lomi massage, which was a much-needed break from our busy lives. The book's advice on "Hawaiian time" was a gentle reminder to slow down and truly savor every moment together.

-Amazon Reviewer

MAUI-If you're planning a trip to **Maui**, "Maui Travel and Adventure Guide" by Ocean Breeze Adventures is an absolute must-read. This book is packed with amazing tips and insights that have significantly helped me prepare for my upcoming trip. The guide is meticulously organized, making it easy to find information on everything, from the best places to stay to the most thrilling activities to try.

What sets this book apart is its focus on providing authentic experiences. The authors clearly have a deep love and understanding of **Maui**, and they share their knowledge in a way that makes you feel like you're getting insider tips from a local. The sections on cultural experiences and local cuisine were particularly enlightening, offering a deeper appreciation for the island's rich heritage and vibrant community.

The adventure tips are comprehensive and cater to all kinds of travelers. Whether you're into hiking, snorkeling, or simply lounging on the beach, this guide covers it all. The detailed descriptions and practical advice ensure that you can make the most of your time on the island, avoiding common tourist pitfalls and discovering hidden gems.

Overall, "Maui Travel and Adventure Guide" is more than just a travel guide—it's a companion that enhances your journey, making your trip to Maui truly unforgettable. I highly recommend this book to anyone looking to experience the best of what Maui has to offer.

Amazon Reviewer

Pack for Paradise

I wanted to thank you for putting your Hawaii travel trust in me. Please grab this Ultimate Hawaii Packing List. You can print it off so you don't forget any essentials!

Most of us can't take our paperback books on vacation. How does an MP3 version of my Oahu Travel Adventure Guide sound? All I ask for in return is to have the best adventures! Mahalo(Thankyou), Diana.

This scan takes you to the sign-up form to grab your fun stuff. Clickable!

Free Stuff

Welcome to Kauai

Life is either a daring adventure or nothing. – Helen Keller

Traveling to Kauai is an invitation to experience a tropical paradise brimming with lush landscapes, pristine beaches, and a vibrant culture deeply rooted in its rich history. Known as the "Garden Isle," Kauai enchants visitors with its stunning natural beauty. Imagine cascading waterfalls, turquoise waters, and dramatic cliffs like those along the Na Pali Coast, creating a visual feast that feels straight out of a dream.

Kauai's allure extends beyond its natural wonders. The island's Hollywood history has made it a favorite backdrop for numerous films, including iconic movies like Jurassic Park, Pirates of the Caribbean, and South Pacific. This cinematic heritage adds an extra layer of intrigue and charm to the island, making it even more captivating for visitors.

What truly sets Kauai apart is its authenticity and the vibrant culture of its people. Unlike more commercialized destinations, Kauai offers a serene and less crowded environment, allowing visitors to fully immerse themselves in the island's unique charm. From exploring quaint towns and local markets to engaging in traditional Hawaiian activities, every moment spent on Kauai promises a genuine and enriching experience.

Kauai's reputation as a best-kept secret makes it a must-visit destination for travelers seeking both adventure and tranquility. Whether you are hiking through emerald valleys, lounging on sun-kissed beaches, or marveling at the island's cinematic landscapes, Kauai offers a truly unforgettable escape.

Chapter One

'Imi ola Kauai (To Search for a Fulfilling Life or Purpose)

Have you ever heard of 'Imi ola Kauai? It is a lot more than just a phrase; it is a quest for a meaningful life, and where better to embark on such a journey than the island of Kauai? This chapter is not just a guide; it is a love letter to this lush paradise and its rich history. Picture this: more beaches than you can count, each with its own unique charm waiting to be explored. But hold on, because Kauai is not just about sunny skies and sandy shores; it is also the reigning champ of rain, earning the title of the wettest place on Earth. And if you think that is impressive, wait until you hear about its thriving coffee scene. Kauai boasts the largest coffee plantation in the entire US. So, whether you are here for the sun, the rain, or just a really good cup of joe, Kauai's got you covered.

Overview of the Garden Isle

Kauai holds the title of "Garden Isle" for a reason. Picture-perfect landscapes, from lush valleys to dramatic cliffs, draw travelers from across the globe to this paradise. It is not just about the stunning scenery; Kauai packs a punch when it comes to unique features and experiences. First off, let's talk size. Kauai might be the fourth-largest island in Hawaii, but do not let its ranking fool you. It is still a cozy 562.3 square miles of pure beauty. Within that relatively small space, you will find wonders that seem to defy the imagination.

Ever heard of Waimea Canyon? If not, prepare to be awestruck. The mighty Waimea River carved this magnificent chasm, which plunges an impressive 3,600 feet into the ground, painting the surroundings in vibrant red and orange hues that can leave you in awe. Then there's the Na Pali Coast, a rugged stretch of shoreline that looks like something straight out of a fantasy novel. Towering sea cliffs, lush valleys, and hidden beaches await those adventurous enough to explore its rugged terrain. And let's not forget Mount Wai'ale'ale, a name that is as impressive as the mountain itself. This towering peak holds the title of one of the wettest spots on Earth, with over 400 inches of rain annually. So, if you are planning a visit, you might want to pack an umbrella!

Waterfalls? From the majestic Wailua Falls to the picturesque Opaekaa Falls, there is no shortage of natural beauty to behold on this island paradise. Now, here's a fun fact for you: Kauai is the only major Hawaiian island without mongooses roaming around. Yes, you heard that right. And you know what else sets it apart? Unlike its island siblings, Kauai does not boast diverse climatic zones or bustling nightlife scenes. Instead, it is a place where you come to unwind, reconnect with nature, and experience the true essence of Hawaii. Speaking of unique features, did you know that Kauai is home to the only navigable river in the Hawaiian Islands? That is right—the Wailua River meanders through lush valleys and ancient forests, offering visitors a serene and unforgettable journey through the heart of the island.

Let's not forget about coffee. Kauai is home to the largest coffee plantation in the entire United States, where acres of verdant fields yield some of the finest beans you will ever taste. So, if you are a caffeine lover, this is one stop you would not want to miss. But perhaps one of the most fascinating aspects of Kauai is its rich cultural heritage. This island is the ancestral home of the mystical Menehune, legendary beings said to be skilled craftsmen and guardians of the land. Their legacy lives on in the stories and traditions passed down through generations, adding an extra layer of magic to an already enchanting destination. Now, let's talk, people. Kauai might be a paradise for visitors, but it is also home to around 73,000 residents who call this island paradise their own. With tourism being a major industry, welcoming over one million visitors annually, the local community plays a vital role in preserving Kauai's natural beauty and cultural heritage.

So, whether you are seeking adventure, relaxation, or a bit of both, Kauai has something for everyone. From its breathtaking landscapes to its rich history and vibrant culture, the Garden Isle invites you to experience the beauty and wonder of Hawaii like never before.

Introduction to Kauai's History

Kauai's history is not just a chronicle of events but an epic tale woven with threads of adventure, cultural exchange, and the spirit of its people against the backdrop of awe-inspiring natural beauty. Let's embark on a journey through time, exploring the captivating narrative that has shaped this island paradise from its ancient origins to its modern-day allure. Picture the vast expanse of the Pacific Ocean, with remote islands scattered like jewels in the sea. Using the stars and their understanding of the winds and currents, Polynesian navigators set out on a perilous journey over thousands of miles of open water around 1500 years ago. Their outrigger canoes carried them to the shores of what we now know as Hawaii, including the landscapes of Kauai. Here, they found a land of lush valleys, cascading waterfalls, and fertile plains—a paradise waiting to be explored.

But Kauai's story did not end with their arrival. Around 500 years later, a second wave of travelers, this time from Tahiti, made landfall on the shores of the island. With them came new beliefs, traditions, and the foundation of what would become Hawaiian culture as we know it today. It is from this Tahitian influence that the pantheon of Hawaiian gods emerged, along with a rich tapestry of myths and legends that continue to resonate with the island's inhabitants. Now, let us talk names. Kauai's name may seem mysterious, but according to legend, it is tied to the Polynesian explorer Hawaii loa, who supposedly named the island after his favorite son. While the origins of its name may be filled with myth, one thing is certain: Kauai holds a special place in the hearts of its people, who strive to preserve the ancient Hawaiian dialect and cultural heritage that define their identity.

Let's fast-forward to the late 1700s, when James Cook, a renowned explorer, led European traders to the Hawaiian Islands. Cook's arrival marked the beginning of a new chapter in Kauai's history, as European influence and trade began to shape the island's destiny. Despite these encounters, Kauai remained relatively untouched compared to its island neighbors. All thanks in part to its resistance against the reign of King Kamehameha, who sought to unite the group of islands under his rule. Speaking of resistance, Kauai's refusal to submit to Kamehameha's authority led to some dramatic showdowns, including two failed attempts by the king to conquer the island. Eventually, a truce was presented, and Kauai's ruler, King Kaumualii, allied with Kamehameha to maintain peace and prevent further conflict.

But Kauai's story does not end there. As the sugar and pineapple industries flourished in the 19th century, immigrants from around the world flocked to the island, bringing with them their own cultural traditions and contributing to the vibrant tapestry of Kauai's multicultural society. These industries fueled the economy until the mid-20th century, when labor strikes and shifting global markets ushered in a new era of change. Kauai evolved once again, this time into a bustling hub of tourism and filmmaking. With its breathtaking landscapes and beaches, the island became a magnet for travelers seeking sun, surf, and a taste of paradise. Today, Kauai stands as a testament to the resilience of its people and the enduring allure of Hawaii's Garden Isle. So, whether you are exploring its lush jungles, marveling at its cliffs, or simply soaking up the sun on its pristine shores, remember that every inch of Kauai is steeped in history—a history that continues to shape the island's vibrant culture and captivating charm. From ancient voyages to modern adventures, Kauai's story is one of resilience, diversity, and the enduring spirit of aloha.

As we wrap up this journey through Kauai's captivating history, it is clear that this island is more than just a tropical paradise; it is a living testament to resilience, cultural exchange, and the enduring spirit of its people. From the ancient voyages of Polynesian navigators to the modern-day allure of tourism and filmmaking, Kauai's story is one of evolution and adaptation in the face of change. But our exploration is far from over. In the next chapter, we will delve deeper into the island's unique character, uncovering hidden gems, local traditions, and insider tips for making the most of your time in this enchanting destination. So, whether you are a first-time visitor or a seasoned traveler, get ready to discover the true essence of Kauai—a place where every corner holds a story waiting to be told.

Chapter Two

Getting to Know Kauai

Wherever you go becomes a part of you somehow. – Anita Desai

I n this chapter, we will dive deep into the heart and soul of this mesmerizing island. From its diverse geography to its unique climate and vibrant culture, we are here to give you the inside scoop on all things Kauai. Whether you are a first-time visitor eager to explore every hidden corner or a seasoned traveler looking to deepen your understanding, this chapter is your ultimate guide to unlocking the essence of Kauai. Get ready to immerse yourself in lush jungles, pristine beaches, and breathtaking vistas as we navigate the landscape of this enchanting destination. From the towering cliffs of the Na Pali Coast to the waters of the Wailua River, each corner of Kauai has its own story to tell. So, grab your sunscreen and your sense of adventure!

Geography

Kauai, the oldest gem in Hawaii's necklace of islands, boasts a stunning blend of natural wonders that earned it the nickname "Garden Island." Picture this: a circular paradise covering roughly 550 square miles, packed with volcanic drama, rainforest majesty, and a coastline that's nothing short of breathtaking. Let's start with Kawaikini Peak, standing tall at 5,148 feet and reigning over Kauai as its highest point. It is a rain magnet, known as one of the wettest spots on the planet, with an impressive 400 inches of rainfall annually. Speaking of impressive, there is nothing quite like the Napali Coast and Waimea Canyon State Park, which steal the show as two of Kauai's most jaw-dropping sights. Zoom out a bit, and you will see that Kauai is not just any island; it is part of a majestic volcanic family, including Big Island, Maui, Oahu, and the rest. This chain stretches across the vastness of the Pacific, standing as a testament to the power of geological forces. It is one of the most isolated island chains globally, with a whopping 350-mile stretch of volcanic peaks rising from the ocean's depths.

Now, let's talk about the magic behind it all—the hot spot. Picture molten magma bubbling up from the Earth's core, shaping these islands over the past 70 million years. It is like a geological movie, creating new mountains while the old guard drifts away. Mauna Kea and Mauna Loa almost touch the stars, outrunning even Mount Everest when you count their underwater roots. Now, let us zero in on Kauai itself. As the elder island of the Hawaiian family, it has been around the block a few times. Erosion has worked its magic, sculpting once-conical volcanoes into the lush wonderland we see today. And with over 400 inches of rain annually, it is no wonder this island is the embodiment of green. But wait, there is more! The weather systems here are not just for show. Those northern Pacific storms sculpt the iconic cliffs of the Na Pali Coast while the trade winds play conductor to a symphony of rainfall. It is this dance of wind and water that carves Kauai into a geographical masterpiece, boasting more freshwater streams than all the other islands combined.

Let's not forget about the neighbors. Niihau, filled with mystery and tradition, stands as a testament to a past era, while Lehua and Kaula are tiny dots in the vastness of the Pacific. Kauai is the crown jewel of Kauai County, covering over 90% of its land area and offering a playground for adventurers and nature lovers alike. From the lush forests of Waialeale to the rugged cliffs of the Na Pali Coast, Kauai is a canvas painted with the brushstrokes of nature's finest work. So whether you are paddling down the Wailua River or hiking through Waimea Canyon, one thing is for sure: there is no place on Earth quite like the Garden Isle.

Climate

Kauai can be regarded as the land of sunshine and gentle breezes. Well, maybe not exactly, but close enough! If you are planning a trip to this paradise, you are in for a treat. From hiking through verdant rainforests to catching waves on pristine beaches, Kauai's climate sets the stage for outdoor adventures of all kinds. So, what's the deal with Kauai's weather? Unlike some places with four distinct seasons, Kauai keeps it simple with just two: summer and winter. There's not a bad time to visit this island gem. Summer, stretching from May to October, brings warmer temperatures and plenty of sunshine. Imagine yourself lounging on a sandy beach, soaking up the rays with a refreshing drink in hand. With surface water temperatures around 82 degrees Fahrenheit in August and September, it is prime time for swimming and snorkeling

But hold onto your sun hat—summer isn't all smooth sailing. July can get a bit breezy, with winds picking up to around 15 miles per hour. And let's not forget about hurricane season, lurking from early June to late November. While major storms like Hurricane Iniki in 1992 are rare, it is always wise to keep an eye on the forecast. Now, let's talk about winter, spanning from November to April. While temperatures might dip slightly, do not expect anything too drastic. Even in January, the coldest month, you are looking at a comfortable 65 degrees Fahrenheit. But what really makes winter special on Kauai? There is lots of rain. Kauai's lush greenery owes much of its beauty to regular rainfall. Mount Waialeale, the island's second-highest peak, is practically a rain magnet, earning its name as one of the wettest spots on Earth.

If you are looking to stay away from the drops, consider setting up camp on the island's drier south side, perhaps in Poipu. But a little rain never hurts anyone, right? Embrace the wetter side of life on the north shore, where beautiful scenery and a laid-back vibe await. Despite its small size, Kauai boasts a surprising diversity of microclimates. Just because it is raining in one spot does not mean it is a washout everywhere else. So, pack your bags and get ready to chase the sun across this island paradise. There's more. If you are feeling adventurous, consider visiting during the holidays. Picture swapping snow for sand and celebrating Christmas with a tropical twist. Do not worry about packing your parka; light jackets will do just fine for those slightly chillier evenings.

Whether you are basking in the summer sun or dancing in the rain, Kauai's climate sets the stage for unforgettable experiences. So, grab your swimsuit and sense of adventure, and get ready to explore all that this island paradise has to offer. Keep in mind that, no matter the weather, there is something magical about Kauai that keeps travelers coming back time and time again. So, embrace the elements, soak up the scenery, and let the spirit of Aloha guide you on your journey through this tropical paradise.

Flora and Fauna

Kauai, also known as the Garden Island, is like a living, breathing Eden, bursting with biodiversity at every turn. Its lush landscapes and pristine ecosystems harbor some of the most unique and fascinating plants and animals on the planet. So buckle up, because we are about to take you on a journey through the incredible flora and fauna of Kauai. What sets Kauai apart from its siblings in the Hawaiian island chain? Well, for starters, it boasts the highest level of diversity among all eight islands. And here's the kicker: It is all because of Kauai's seniority. It is the oldest Hawaiian island in the bunch.

Let us dive into the plant kingdom first. Imagine yourself strolling through a botanical wonderland where every bloom tells a story of evolution and adaptation. Here on Kauai, you will encounter some real showstoppers, like the plumeria, orchids, hibiscus, and the ohia tree. The plumeria, also known as Frangipani, is like a fragrant beacon, drawing you in with its sweet scent and vibrant hues. And do not be surprised if you find yourself adorned with a lei made from its velvety petals—it is a Hawaiian tradition, after all. Next up, Orchids. Kauai is a paradise for orchid enthusiasts, with its diverse climate zones providing the perfect habitat for these delicate beauties. From the roadside to the rainforest, you will find an array of orchids in every color of the rainbow.

Who could forget the Hibiscus, Hawaii's state flower? These trumpet-shaped blooms add a splash of tropical color to Kauai's landscapes, lining roadsides and gardens with their vibrant presence. Last but not least, the Ohia Tree stands tall as a symbol of Hawaii's native flora. With its fiery red blossoms and glossy green leaves, it is a sight to behold in Kauai's forests, playing a vital role in the island's ecosystem.

Now, let's talk fauna. Kauai's wildlife is just as captivating as its plant life, with a cast of characters that includes some real gems. First up is the Hawaiian Monk Seal. As one of the rarest seal species in the world, spotting one of these beauties basking on the beach is a real treat. And then there's the Nene Goose, Hawaii's state bird, with its distinctive appearance. But that's not all. The Kauai Elepaio, with its charming song, adds a musical touch to the island's forests while dolphins dive in the surrounding seas, delighting visitors with their playful antics. And let's not forget about the "wild" domesticated chickens that roam the island, adding a touch of whimsy to Kauai's rural landscape.

But perhaps what's most remarkable about Kauai's flora and fauna is its resilience. Despite centuries of change, from ancient trade routes to modern tourism, Kauai's natural treasures continue to thrive, offering sanctuary to endangered species and delighting visitors with their beauty. So, whether you're a nature lover, a birdwatcher, or simply someone who appreciates the wonders of the natural world, Kauai is a paradise waiting to be explored. And what better way to start than by immersing yourself in the island's botanical gardens, where every plant tells a story of survival and adaptation?

Cultural Background of Kauai and the People of Hawaii

Let's have a look at the cultural background of Kauai and what you can expect once you visit this island paradise.

Hula

Hawaii is not just about stunning landscapes and sunny beaches. It is a cultural melting pot with a rich and vibrant history. At the heart of Hawaiian culture is hula, an art form that's so much more than just dancing. It is a way of storytelling, a way of preserving traditions, and a way of connecting with the land and its people. Hula comes in two main flavors: Hula Kahiko and Hula Auana. Hula Kahiko is the OG, developed long before Europeans set foot on Hawaiian shores. It is steeped in tradition, with movements and chants that tell the stories of ancient Hawaii. On the flip side, Hula Auana emerged later, blending Hawaiian tradition with European and American influences. It is a more contemporary take on hula, with music, costumes, and choreography that reflect Hawaii's evolving cultural landscape.

Then there is the Merrie Monarch Festival, the biggest of all hula celebrations. Held annually in Hilo on the Big Island, it is a week-long extravaganza of dance, music, and cultural pride. Hula troupes from across the islands come together to showcase their skills, paying homage to the ancestors who paved the way. But hula is just the tip of the cultural iceberg in Hawaii. From the language to the cuisine to the traditional arts and crafts, Hawaii's cultural tapestry is as diverse as its people. With influences from Polynesia, Asia, Europe, and beyond, it's a testament to the island's history of migration and exploration. Whether you are swaying to the rhythm of the hula or feasting on a plate of kalua pig, remember that Hawaii's cultural heritage is alive and thriving. It is a celebration of diversity, resilience, and the spirit of aloha that binds people together.

Voyaging and Navigation

Picture this: You are out on the open ocean, with nothing but the vast expanse of blue stretching out before you. Imagine navigating your way across that ocean using nothing but the stars, the wind, and the motion of the waves. It sounds like something out of a movie, right? Well, for the Polynesian voyagers who first settled in Hawaii, it was just another day at sea. These ancient seafarers were skilled navigators, using their keen senses and deep knowledge of the natural world to guide their double-hulled canoes across the Pacific. They did not have fancy GPS systems or maps. They relied on the stars to show them the way, the winds to fill their sails, and the currents to carry them to their destination.

But the art of Polynesian navigation did not die out with the voyagers of old. Organizations like the Polynesian Voyaging Society are keeping the tradition alive, working tirelessly to preserve the ancient knowledge and sailing techniques that allowed their ancestors to traverse the ocean with such precision. It is not just about preserving history; it is about honoring it. By passing down the skills of navigation to future generations, these organizations are ensuring that the spirit of exploration and adventure lives on. It is a reminder that even in our modern world of technology and convenience, there's still something to be said for the wisdom of the past.

Religion and Spirituality

Did you know that Hawaiian spirituality is deeply rooted in the land and the family? Yes, it is all about connecting with the natural world and honoring your ancestors. So, back in the day, before the missionaries rolled in, the traditional Hawaiian religion was all about polytheism and animism. They had a whole squad of gods, like Kane, Kanaloa, Kū, and Lono, each with their own domain and powers. And let's not forget about Pele, the fiery volcano goddess who's a big deal around these parts. But here's the thing: it is not just about praying to the gods and goddesses. It is about respecting the land ('āina) and your family ('ohana). These are like the core principles of Hawaiian spirituality. The land is seen as a living, breathing entity, and taking care of it is seen as a sacred duty. Family is everything. It is about honoring your ancestors and passing down their wisdom and traditions to future generations.

You can see these beliefs reflected in Hawaiian culture and practices. From the way they care for the land to the way they celebrate special occasions with their families, it is all connected to their spiritual beliefs. Even today, Hawaiian spirituality continues to shape the cultural values of the islands. It is a reminder of the importance of living in harmony with the natural world and staying connected to your roots. The next time you are in Hawaii, take a moment to appreciate the spiritual side of the islands. Whether you are hiking through the lush rainforests or enjoying a family meal on the beach, you are experiencing a culture that's deeply rooted in tradition and reverence for the land and the family.

Music and Arts

Have you ever listened to Hawaiian music? It is like a tropical vibe for your ears, full of soul and rhythm. Mele, which is a Hawaiian poem and song, is a big deal here. They are not just music; they are a way of telling stories, sharing history, and expressing feelings. Then there are oli, which are chants. They are like ancient prayers, passed down through generations, with each word carrying its own power and meaning. It is pretty mesmerizing to listen to, especially when you are surrounded by the beauty of the islands.

But it is not just about the words. It is about the instruments too. Ever heard of the ukulele? Yeah, that tiny little guitar with the big sound. It is like the unofficial mascot of Hawaiian music, bringing joy and melody wherever it goes. Let's not forget about the slack-key guitar, a local favorite that's been making waves around the world. But music is just one piece of the puzzle when it comes to Hawaiian arts. The islands are bursting with creativity, from visual arts like painting and sculpture to performance arts like hula and traditional dance. There are cultural institutions dedicated to preserving and celebrating these art forms, showcasing the talent and diversity of Hawaiian culture.

Land and Society

Hawaii was divided into these things called moku and ahupua'a. Moku were like these big districts, and ahupua'a were smaller sections within them. Each ahupua'a stretched from the mountains to the sea, which meant that people had access to all different kinds of resources, from freshwater streams to ocean fish. But here is where it gets interesting: the whole social structure was tied to this land tenure system. One's place in society was determined by where they lived and what resources they had access to. It was like a caste system, with different social roles and responsibilities depending on which ahupua'a you were in. Land and family were everything in Hawaiian culture. Connection to the land was sacred, and taking care of it was seen as a sacred duty.

Now that you are aware of the culture and people of Kauai, it is time that we start our journey to the magical island of Kauai. Flip the page to learn more!

Chapter Three

Planning a Trip to Paradise

There is a kind of magicness about going far away and then coming back all changed. – Kate Douglas Wiggin

Thinking about planning a trip to paradise? Well, you are in for a treat! In this chapter, we are diving into all things Kauai, the Garden Isle of Hawaii. Whether you are a seasoned traveler or a first-time adventurer, we have got you covered with everything you need to know to make your trip to Kauai unforgettable. From stunning landscapes to vibrant culture, Kauai has something for everyone. But before you pack your bags and jet off to this tropical paradise, there are a few things you will want to consider. It is time to turn your dream vacation into a reality!

How to Get to Kauai

Dreaming of a getaway to Kauai? You are not alone! Before you dive into planning, let's talk about how to get there. With its stunning beaches and lush landscapes, Kauai is a hot spot for travelers worldwide. But navigating your way to this tropical paradise requires a bit of information. From flights to ferry rides, we have a breakdown of your transportation options.

By Plane

Kauai, known for its stunning landscapes and serene beaches, welcomes you through Lihue Airport. It is the island's sole commercial aviation hub, located on the east side. If you are flying from the US or Canada, you are in luck with direct flights. But for others, a connecting flight is the key. Now, if your journey involves a layover, fear not. Hawaii's interconnected islands offer a smooth transition. Simply get on a 20-minute flight from Honolulu International or other major Hawaiian airports, and you will be at Lihue Airport. Aim for just one connection to Kauai for smoother travel. East Coasters, consider a direct flight to Oahu, saving you a precious couple of hours. Meanwhile, West Coasters have the luxury of flying straight to Kauai, cutting down on transit time. When it comes to airlines, Hawaiian Airlines is well-known for its friendly service. It is your golden ticket to Kauai, especially with direct routes from the West Coast and Vegas. Plus, Hawaiian Airlines opens doors to Kauai from the East Coast via Oahu. Other airlines include Alaska Airlines, American Airlines, Delta, United, and Southwest.

By Cruise Ship

Getting to Kauai by cruise ship might not be as mainstream as catching a flight, but it is definitely an option worth considering. Picture yourself sailing across the vast expanse of the Pacific Ocean, with each wave bringing you closer to the lush greenery and breathtaking scenery of Kauai. Transpacific cruises that include stops at the Hawaiian islands offer a unique and leisurely way to experience the beauty of Kauai. You will get to soak up the sun, enjoy the sea breeze, and indulge in the luxurious amenities of your cruise ship while making your way to the Garden Isle. While the journey might take a bit longer compared to flying, the experience itself is unforgettable. You will have the chance to explore multiple destinations along the way, making the voyage to Kauai an adventure in itself.

By Boat

Presently, reaching Kauai by boat is not an option on the table. Your best bet for getting to and from the island is by plane. Once you have touched down in Kauai via air travel, the ocean adventures are far from over. You can embrace the island spirit and dive into various kinds of boat trips. Whether you crave a romantic evening under the hues of the sunset or seek a family-friendly escape to witness majestic whales and vibrant marine life, Kauai offers a wide range of boat excursions tailored to every type of traveler.

Planning Your Trip

Are you all set to visit Kauai? Here are some recommendations that can help.

Best Time to Visit

For optimal weather, fewer crowds, and better prices, aim for Kauai in the spring (April–May) or fall (August–October). These shoulder seasons boast pleasant conditions and fewer tourists compared to the peak winter and summer months. Winter (November–March) may bring more rain and higher prices, but it is ideal for spotting humpback whales. Summer (June–July) brings busier crowds and higher costs, yet rewards with fantastic beach weather. Consider your preferences and priorities to pick the perfect time for your Kauai adventure.

Budgeting and Expenses

When it comes to budgeting for a trip to Kauai, timing is key. Opt for the spring and fall shoulder seasons for lower airfare and hotel rates. Avoid the peak winter and summer seasons when prices skyrocket, especially around holidays. Be prepared for increased expenses compared to pre-pandemic times, with airfare and rental car costs running 20%–35% higher due to inflation. To stretch your budget further, consider staying in budget accommodations like hostels or guesthouses instead of high-end resorts. Utilize public transportation or carpooling to save on rental car costs. Explore local eateries and markets for affordable dining options rather than dining at upscale restaurants. On average, expect to spend around $150-$300 per day per person for mid-range expenses, including accommodation, meals, transportation, and activities. However, costs can vary widely depending on your preferences and travel style. With careful planning and smart spending, you can enjoy the beauty of Kauai without breaking the bank.

Accommodation Options

Kauai offers a diverse array of accommodation choices catering to every traveler's preference. From luxury resorts to cozy vacation rentals and charming Airbnbs, there is something for everyone. For peace of mind, it is wise to secure your accommodation well in advance, especially if you are planning to visit during peak travel periods. This ensures you grab the best deals and have a wide selection to choose from. To enhance your Kauai experience, consider exploring different regions of the island for accommodation. Each area boasts its own unique microclimate and scenery. Whether you are drawn to the lush landscapes of the north shore or the sunny shores of the south shore, branching out allows you to fully immerse yourself in Kauai's natural beauty. Stay tuned for special recommendations in the upcoming chapters, tailored to help you find the perfect place to rest your head during your Kauai getaway.

Transportation on the Island

When it comes to getting around Kauai, having reliable transportation is key to fully experiencing the island's diverse landscapes and attractions. Renting a car is highly recommended, offering the flexibility to explore at your own pace and venture off the beaten path. With a rental car, you can easily navigate Kauai's scenic coastal highways, winding mountain roads, and hidden gems tucked away in remote corners of the island. Plus, it provides the freedom to embark on spontaneous adventures and discover hidden beaches, picturesque waterfalls, and breathtaking viewpoints. Stay tuned for special recommendations in the upcoming chapters, where we will delve deeper into transportation options on the island.

Kauai has a lot to offer when it comes to traveling. In the next section, we will dive into travel essentials such as immigration and restrictions. Learning about travel restrictions and rules can ensure that you have a smooth traveling experience as you visit the island paradise. Stay tuned to learn more!

Chapter Four

Talking About Ho'omana (Empowerment)

To travel is to discover that everyone is wrong about other countries. – Aldous Huxley

Navigating the complexity of customs and immigration laws can feel like a daunting task, but it does not have to be. In this chapter, we are diving into Ho'omana empowerment to help you confidently manage these challenges. We will break down the essential steps and guidelines to ensure you are fully compliant with importation and immigration regulations. Whether you are traveling for business, relocating, or simply bringing in goods from abroad, understanding these rules is crucial. So, let us demystify the process and empower you with the knowledge to handle customs and immigration with ease and assurance.

Understanding Agricultural Restrictions

Understanding agricultural restrictions is crucial when traveling to Hawaii, including Kauai. The unique ecosystem of the islands is highly vulnerable, and the Hawaii Department of Agriculture (HDOA) strictly enforces regulations to prevent the introduction of invasive species and plant diseases. Here is a closer look at what you need to know.

Restricted or Prohibited Items

While most plants can enter Hawaii after inspection, several items are either restricted or prohibited unless you make prior arrangements for permits, quarantine, treatments, or certifications. These include:

- **Pineapple and Bromeliad Plants and Fruits:** These are common but restricted without proper certification.

- **Passion Fruit Plants and Seeds:** Similarly restricted to prevent the spread of pests and diseases.

- **Cruciferous Root Vegetables:** Items like radish, turnip, daikon, horseradish, and rutabaga require special handling.

- **Corn on the Cob:** Needs prior arrangement before shipping to Hawaii.

- **Citrus and Pulpy Fruits from Florida and Puerto Rico:** Must be treated or certified due to the risk of invasive species.

- **Taro and Dasheen:** Common in Hawaiian cuisine but regulated for import.

- **Coconuts:** Coconuts are also on the list of restricted items.

- **Orchid Plants:** These beautiful plants require an import permit and certificate of origin.

- **Plants in the Grass Family:** Including sugar cane and bamboo, need special permits.

- **Coffee Plants and Plant Parts:** Including seeds, which must be fumigated and certified before shipment.

- **Palm Plants:** are restricted for their potential to carry pests.

- **Certain Flowering Plants:** Aster, chrysanthemum, hollyhock, dahlia, and gladiolus plants require certification.

- **Pine Plants and Parts:** Need certification, but cut branches are allowed between October 20 and December 31.

- **Sorghum, Broomcorn, and Sudan Grass:** Non-propagative parts need certification; propagative parts require permits and quarantine.

Food Products

Generally, foods that are cooked, canned, frozen, or commercially processed and packaged can be transported to Hawaii if they originate from within the U.S. This includes:

- **Frozen or Chilled Meats:** are allowed as long as they come from within the U.S.

- **Manufactured Food Products:** Do not require declaration or inspection, making it easier to bring packaged goods.

By understanding and adhering to these regulations, you can help protect Hawaii's delicate ecosystem while ensuring a smooth entry process. Whether you are planning to bring plants or food, being informed about these restrictions is essential for a hassle-free experience.

Travel Documents and Copies

When flying to and from Hawaii or traveling between the Hawaiian Islands, the required documents are the same as for any other U.S. state. For domestic flights, a valid government-issued photo ID is all you need. The TSA website provides a comprehensive list of accepted IDs. For children and teenagers under 18 traveling with an adult who has a valid ID, no ID is required. However, it is a good idea for them to carry some form of identification, such as a school ID card. For lap infants, proof of age, such as a copy of the birth certificate, may be requested.

For international travel, including for infants and children, a valid passport is required. Depending on your destination, a visa might also be necessary. Ensuring the safety of these essential documents is crucial during your travels.

- **Make Digital and Physical Copies:** In today's digital age, having digital copies of your travel documents can be a lifesaver. Scan or take clear photos of all your vital documents and email them to yourself. This ensures that they are accessible from anywhere. Additionally, keep photocopies of your documents in separate locations in your luggage. This can be extremely helpful if you lose the originals.

- **Use Plastic Bags:** Protect your travel documents from damage by storing them in plastic zip-lock bags. These bags are waterproof and keep your documents organized. Larger bags can hold items like airline tickets, while smaller ones are perfect for passports and cards. This simple step can save your documents from spills or unexpected rain.

- **Find Secure Storage:** Once you arrive at your hotel, locate a secure storage space for your documents. Most accommodations offer a safe or lockbox in the room. Utilize these to store your original documents when not needed. However, do not forget to retrieve your documents when checking out. If no safe is available, consider storing them in less obvious places, like inside a packed shoe in your suitcase.

Creating a Traveler's Emergency Contact Card

An emergency contact card can be incredibly useful. Here's how to make one:

- **Step 1:** Find a Laminating Tool: A self-laminating tool from a local store or online can make your card durable.

- **Step 2:** Identify What to Put on the Card Include your name, citizenship and passport number, emergency contacts, financial institution toll-free numbers, consular services numbers, and medical insurance information.

- **Step 3:** Create the Document: Use a program like Word or Google Docs to format your information on one or both sides of the card. Ensure it fits within the dimensions of your laminating pocket.

- **Step 4:** Print and Test Print a copy to check the size. Adjust if necessary, then print the required number of copies.

- **Step 5:** Laminate the Cards: Distribute the laminated cards throughout your belongings for easy access by you or anyone assisting you in an emergency. Consider placing them in your travel wallet, phone case, passport sleeve, security belt, outerwear pocket, and each bag.

By taking these steps, you can ensure your travel documents and essential information are safe and accessible throughout your journey.

Navigating Customs and Immigration

Navigating customs and immigration in Kauai can be straightforward if you are well-prepared. Here's what you need to know.

Entry Requirements and Documentation

- **Visa Requirements:** Depending on your nationality, you might need a visa to enter the U.S. Check the U.S. Department of State's website for specific requirements. If you are eligible for the Visa Waiver Program (VWP), you can travel without a visa for stays of up to 90 days. Remember to register with the Electronic System for Travel Authorization (ESTA) before your trip.

- **Passport:** A valid passport is essential. Ensure it is up-to-date and will remain valid for your entire stay. Some countries also require a passport to be valid for several months beyond your departure date, so double-check this before you travel.

- **Customs Information:** When arriving in Kauai, you will need to complete a customs declaration form. This form requires you to declare items you are bringing into the U.S., especially agricultural products, which are subject to strict regulations to protect Hawaii's unique ecosystem. Additionally, you will fill out an immigration form, providing details about your stay and confirming your eligibility to enter the U.S.

Being prepared with the right documentation and understanding the entry requirements will help you breeze through customs and immigration, allowing you to enjoy your time in beautiful Kauai without any hassles. In the next chapter, we will talk about the Hawaiian culture.

Chapter Five

Be Your Own A'Ali'I (Hawaiian Shrub With Small, Fragrant Flowers; Symbol of Strength and Resilience)

It is only in adventure that some people succeed in knowing themselves – in finding themselves. – Andre Gide

Understanding the Hawaiian way of life goes beyond the beautiful land-scapes and vibrant culture. It is about embracing the spirit of Aloha, a guiding principle and even a law in Hawaii. In this chapter, we will delve into the symbolism of the A'ali'i, a resilient shrub, and learn how to embody its strength. We will explore the meaning and importance of the Shaka symbol and guide you through the cultural etiquette expected when visiting these islands. By the end, you will not only appreciate Hawaii's customs but also know how to honor them during your travels.

The Spirit of 'Aloha'

The spirit of 'Aloha' is far more profound than a simple greeting. It embodies the Hawaiian essence of love, compassion, and unity, permeating everyday interactions and cultural practices. In Kauai, this spirit shapes the warm and welcoming nature of its residents, creating a unique and inviting atmosphere.

The Aloha Spirit Law

Did you know the Aloha Spirit is legally recognized in Hawaii? The Aloha Spirit Law, encoded in the Hawaii Revised Statutes, section 5-7.5, enshrines this philosophy as a guiding principle for all citizens and government officials. It requires everyone to act with Aloha in their daily lives and duties, ensuring that the essence of kindness, unity, and respect continues to thrive. This law is not just a symbolic gesture; it is a practical framework for maintaining the unique character of Hawaii. Visitors are also encouraged to embrace this spirit, contributing to the island's harmonious environment. The Aloha Spirit elevates and empowers, making Hawaii a special place where the past's wisdom guides the present and future.

Principles of the Aloha Spirit

The Aloha Spirit involves coordinating mind and heart, fostering positive interactions and creating a sense of community. Here are its core principles:

- **Akahai (Kindness):** Expressed with tenderness, it promotes gentle and considerate actions.

- **Lokahi (Unity):** Emphasized through harmony, it encourages working together and supporting one another.

- **Olu Olu (Agreeableness):** Manifested as pleasantness, it enhances social interactions with warmth and friendliness.

- **Ha aha a (Humility):** Demonstrated through modesty, it values the importance of staying grounded and respectful.

- **Ahonui (Patience):** Shown with perseverance, it underscores the need for understanding and tolerance.

Embracing the Aloha Spirit means making a conscious effort to think and feel positively towards others, enriching the community, and preserving Hawaii's unique cultural heritage. Whether you are a resident or a visitor, living by these principles ensures that the Aloha Spirit remains vibrant and real, creating a legacy of love and compassion for future generations.

The Shaka Sign

The shaka sign, a simple yet powerful hand gesture, is synonymous with Hawaiian culture. Made by extending the thumb and pinky finger while curling the three middle fingers, the shaka is a symbol of goodwill, positivity, and the laid-back island lifestyle that Hawaii is famous for. The origins of the shaka sign are rooted in local legend. One popular story credits the gesture to a Hawaiian fisherman from the early 20th century named Hamana Kalili. After losing the three middle fingers of his hand in an accident, he continued to work, using his distinct hand gesture to signal others that everything was alright. This gesture eventually caught on and spread throughout the islands.

Today, the shaka sign carries various meanings depending on the context. It can be a friendly greeting, a way to say thank you, or simply a gesture to convey the spirit of aloha. When you are on the road in Hawaii and someone lets you merge into traffic, you might see a shaka thrown in appreciation. It is a universal symbol among locals and visitors alike, capturing the essence of island life: relaxed, friendly, and full of positive vibes. The shaka is more than just a hand sign; it embodies the aloha spirit, which is about being kind, helpful, and genuinely caring for others. It is a reflection of Hawaii's culture, where community and connection are paramount. Whether you are surfing the waves, hiking the lush trails, or just enjoying a day at the beach, flashing a shaka is a way to share a moment of joy and connection with those around you. So, next time you are in

Hawaii or even just thinking about it, remember the shaka. It is a small gesture with a big heart, perfectly capturing the essence of Hawaiian life.

Hawaiian Time

Hawaiian time is a concept that embodies the relaxed and flexible approach to scheduling and timekeeping found in the islands. It is all about slowing down, letting go of the rigid structure of daily life, and embracing a more laid-back, stress-free pace. In Hawaii, punctuality takes on a different meaning. Things happen when they happen, and there is no rush to stick to strict schedules. This relaxed attitude encourages people to be present, enjoy the moment, and not stress about the clock. Whether it is a casual get-together, a meeting, or a leisurely activity, the focus is on the experience rather than the exact timing. Visitors to Hawaii often find that adopting Hawaiian time allows them to truly unwind and immerse themselves in the island lifestyle. Instead of rushing from one activity to the next, they can take their time, soak in the beauty of their surroundings, and connect with the local culture. It is an invitation to slow down and appreciate life's simple pleasures.

Preservation of Language

The Hawaiian language, or 'Ōlelo Hawai'i, is crucial in preserving the cultural heritage of the islands. Its revival is more than just a linguistic endeavor; it is a reclaiming of identity and history. Historically, Hawaiian was the primary language for governance, education, and daily life in the islands. However, after Hawaii's annexation by the United States in 1898, English replaced Hawaiian in official settings, leading to a decline in its use. Efforts to revitalize the Hawaiian language have been gaining momentum. In 1978, Hawaiian was re-established as the official language of the state of Hawaii. Educational initiatives followed, with Hawaiian becoming the medium of instruction in selected public schools starting in 1987. These immersion programs have been pivotal in fostering new generations of Hawaiian speakers.

Bilingual signage across the islands also plays a significant role in promoting the language. Seeing Hawaiian alongside English in public spaces serves as a constant reminder of the language's importance and helps integrate it into daily life. Federal support has further bolstered these efforts. In 1990, the U.S. government recognized Hawaii's right to preserve and promote its indigenous language. Today, Hawaiian is the most widely studied Native American language, with a growing number of speakers in homes and schools. This resurgence is not just about preserving words but also keeping the spirit and traditions of Hawaiian culture alive for future generations.

Cultural Etiquette Tips

Appreciating and respecting Hawaiian culture is key when visiting the islands. Here are some cultural etiquette tips to help you engage respectfully with locals and participate in cultural events.

- **Appreciate Lei:** Leis are not just beautiful garlands; they hold deep cultural significance. Since the early Polynesian settlers, leis have symbolized peace, love, and respect. If someone gives you a lei, wear it gracefully around your neck with the flowers hanging down. Do not play with it or wear it on your head. For pregnant women, wearing a lei is considered bad luck as it symbolizes the umbilical cord wrapping around the baby's neck. If you are pregnant, you can politely decline by saying, "I am hapai (pregnant). "

- **Respect Sacred Sites:** Hawaii is home to numerous sacred sites, from temples to ancient petroglyphs. When visiting these areas, speak and walk quietly, and always leave the site as you found it. Avoid picking flowers or rearranging rocks, as these actions can be seen as disrespectful.

- **Surf Like a Local:** Surfing is a cherished activity in Hawaii. If you are a beginner, stay clear of more experienced surfers. Wait your turn and ensure others have caught their waves before attempting yours. Respect the locals and be mindful of others in the water and on the beach.

- **Respect the Kupuna:** Elders, or kupuna, hold a special place in Hawaiian society. Show respect by letting them go ahead of you, holding doors open, and offering your seat if necessary. Respecting elders is always appreciated.

- **Know Aloha and Mahalo:** Learn and use these two important Hawaiian words. "Aloha" means hello, goodbye, and love, while "mahalo" means thank you. Using these words shows respect and appreciation for the local culture.

- **Take Off Your Shoes:** When invited into someone's home, remove your shoes before entering. This custom, brought by Japanese immigrants, is a sign of respect. Place your shoes neatly in line with those of others outside the door.

- **Be a Courteous Driver:** Driving in Hawaii requires a laid-back approach. Avoid aggressive driving and honking. Be courteous, allowing others to merge and ease into traffic.

- **Know What You Can Take:** Avoid taking lava rocks or black sand as souvenirs. Local tradition holds that removing these items brings bad luck. Some people have even mailed items back after experiencing misfortune.

- **Respect Hawaii Wildlife:** Never touch or approach endangered animals like sea turtles, monk seals, and humpback whales. It is both illegal and disrespectful to Hawaiian tradition.

- **Honor Hula:** Hula is a sacred dance that expresses Hawaiian culture and history. If you are at a performance, feel free to join in respectfully, but never mock the dance or dancers. Hula is a serious and cherished art form.

Understanding and honoring these customs will enrich your experience and show your respect for Hawaii's rich cultural heritage. In the next section, we will discuss the north shore of Kauai.

Chapter Six

Getting to the North Shore

P lanning a trip to Kauai's North Shore offers a chance to explore some of the island's most breathtaking scenery. From the lush landscapes of Hanalei Valley to the stunning beaches along the coast, this area is a paradise for nature lovers and adventure seekers alike. Getting to the North Shore involves a scenic drive along the island's main highway, Kuhio Highway (Route 56). The journey itself is part of the experience, as you pass through charming small towns and witness panoramic views of the ocean and mountains. It is a good idea to rent a car to have the flexibility to explore at your own pace, stopping at various lookout points and hidden gems along the way.

In this chapter, you will find detailed information about must-see attractions, tips for navigating the area, and recommendations for places to eat and stay. Whether you are interested in hiking the Nā Pali Coast, relaxing on Hanalei Bay, or simply soaking in the island's natural beauty, the North Shore of Kauai promises an unforgettable adventure.

How to Get to the North Shore of Kauai From Lihue Airport

Traveling from Lihue Airport to the North Shore of Kauai is a delightful journey, with several transportation options to suit different preferences and needs. Whether you choose a shuttle service, rental car, or rideshare, each option has its own benefits.

Shuttle Service

For those who prefer not to drive, shuttle services such as North Shore Cab Co. offer a convenient way to travel from Lihue Airport to the North Shore. These services are reliable and can take you to various destinations in the North Shore area, including popular spots like Princeville. The travel time is approximately 1 hour and 10 minutes, providing a hassle-free way to start your vacation. Shuttles are a great choice if you want to relax and enjoy the scenic drive without the worry of navigating unfamiliar roads.

Rental Car

Renting a car is highly recommended for visitors who want the freedom to explore Kauai at their own pace. Several major rental car companies, such as Hertz, Avis, Budget, and Enterprise, have desks and counters conveniently located right at the Lihue Airport terminal. Picking up a rental car upon arrival is straightforward and efficient, allowing you to hit the road quickly. Driving yourself not only gets you to the North Shore in about an hour and ten minutes but also gives you the flexibility to explore other parts of the island, discover hidden gems, and stop at scenic spots along the way. A rental car is ideal for adventurers who plan to visit multiple locations and enjoy spontaneous excursions.

Rideshare/Taxi

Rideshare services like Uber and Lyft are available for pick-up and drop-off at Lihue Airport, offering another convenient transportation option. While these services can be slightly more limited on the island compared to major cities, they still provide a reliable way to reach the North Shore. The advantage of using rideshare is the ease of arranging a ride directly from your smartphone. Additionally, traditional taxis are available at the airport, though they might be a bit more expensive than rideshare services. Both options are suitable for those who prefer not to drive and want a direct route to their accommodation.

Must-See Destinations

Exploring Kauai's North Shore is a must for any visitor, with a variety of stunning destinations that highlight the island's natural beauty and cultural richness.

- **Nā Pali Coast State Wilderness Park:** This breathtaking coastline is known for its towering sea cliffs, lush valleys, and remote beaches. Accessing this area requires some effort, either by boat or hiking, but the views and serenity are well worth it. The Nā Pali Coast offers some of the most dramatic landscapes in all of Hawaii.

- **Hāʻena State Park:** Hāʻena is home to the famous Kalalau Trail, a challenging yet rewarding hike that offers incredible views of the coastline. The park also features Keʻe Beach, a perfect spot to relax and take in the stunning surroundings. It's a must-visit for those looking to experience Kauai's natural beauty up close.

- **Hanalei Bay:** This large, crescent-shaped bay is ideal for swimming, surfing, and enjoying scenic views. The nearby town of Hanalei is charming, with great shops and restaurants that provide a taste of local culture and cuisine. Hanalei Bay is perfect for both adventure and relaxation.

- **Tunnels Beach:** Known for its excellent snorkeling, Tunnels Beach boasts a vibrant reef teeming with marine life. It is a great spot for underwater exploration and enjoying the colorful sea creatures that inhabit the area.

- **Anini Beach:** Anini offers a serene setting with lots of shade and calm waters, making it ideal for spotting sea turtles while snorkeling. This beach is perfect for a relaxing day by the water.

- **Kilauea Lighthouse:** Perched at the northernmost point of the island, Kilauea Lighthouse offers stunning ocean views and is a great spot for bird-watching. The lighthouse is an iconic symbol of Kauai and provides a glimpse into the island's maritime history.

- **NaAina Kai Botanical Gardens:** Spread over 240 acres, these botanical gardens are a feast for the senses. With diverse plant life and beautiful sculptures, NaAina Kai is a wonderful place to explore and enjoy the beauty of nature.

Places to Stay on North Shore

Exploring the North Shore of Kauai means you will need a great place to stay. Here are some top choices, ranging from budget-friendly options to premium accommodations.

Princeville Area

- **The Cliffs at Princeville:** This mid-range resort offers stunning ocean views and spacious suites. Prices range from $200 to $350 per night. It is perfect for families and those looking for a blend of comfort and affordability.

- **The Westin Princeville Ocean Resort Villas:** For a more luxurious stay, the Westin offers upscale villas with full kitchens and private balconies. Prices start around $400 per night and can go up to $800, providing a premium experience with resort amenities.

- **Vacation Rentals in the Villas of Kamali'i at Princeville:** These vacation rentals offer a home-like atmosphere with multiple bedrooms, making them ideal for families or groups. Prices typically range from $250 to $450 per night, depending on the size and location of the villa.

Hanalei Bay Area

- **1 Hotel Hanalei Bay:** This eco-friendly, luxury hotel offers breath-taking views of Hanalei Bay and is perfect for those seeking a high-end experience. Rooms start at around $600 per night, making it one of the more premium options on the North Shore.

- **Hanalei Colony Resort:** Located right on the beach, this resort offers a serene and secluded experience. With rates ranging from $250 to $450 per night, it provides a peaceful retreat with direct access to the beach and beautiful ocean views.

Other North Shore Options

- **Kaha Lani Resort in Lihue:** Though not exactly on the North Shore, this resort offers great value, with prices ranging from $150 to $300 per night. It is a bit further away but offers easy access to many North Shore attractions.

- **The West Inn Kauai in Waimea:** Another slightly further option, this inn offers budget-friendly accommodations starting at around $100 per night. It is ideal for travelers who want to save on lodging while still being within driving distance of the North Shore's highlights.

These options cater to various budgets and preferences, ensuring you find the perfect place to stay while exploring the beautiful North Shore of Kauai.

Places to Eat at North Shore Kauai

Exploring the North Shore of Kauai offers a variety of dining options to satisfy any craving. From budget-friendly spots to premium restaurants, here are some top picks.

- **Harvest Market Natural Foods and Cafe (Hanalei):** Perfect for health-conscious eaters, this market offers organic and natural groceries, a hot bar, deli items, and a salad bar. Prices are reasonable, with most meals costing around $10–$15. It is a great place to grab a nutritious meal to enjoy at a nearby beach.

- **Postcards Cafe (Hanalei):** This charming cafe brings a touch of Old Hawaii with vintage decor and delicious dishes. The menu features fresh produce and seafood, with standout items like taro fritters and grilled fish. Expect to spend around $20–$35 per person. Reservations are recommended for a delightful dining experience.

- **Kilauea Bakery & Pau Hana Pizza (Kilauea):** Known for its baked goods and gourmet pizzas, this bakery is a perfect stop for breakfast or lunch. Enjoy pastries, sourdough bread, and innovative pizzas for around $10–$20 per meal. Outdoor seating is available in the shopping center.

- **Hanalei Taro & Juice Co. (Hanalei):** This local favorite serves traditional Hawaiian food with a modern twist from a lunch wagon. Try their taro smoothies, Hawaiian plate lunches, and taro veggie burgers. Meals here are budget-friendly, typically costing between $10 and $15.

- **Hanalei Dolphin Restaurant and Fish Market (Hanalei):** With a fish market next door, this restaurant specializes in fresh seafood. Enjoy dishes like baked shrimp, ceviche, and crab along the river. While on the pricier side, with meals ranging from $30 to $50, the quality and ambiance are worth it.

- **Kilauea Fish Market (Kilauea):** This casual spot offers fresh local fish, ahi fajita burritos, fish tacos, and more. Prices are generally affordable, around $10–$20 per meal. It is a great place for a quick and delicious lunch, with outdoor picnic table seating.

- **Bar Acuda Tapas & Wine (Hanalei):** For a more upscale experience, Bar Acuda offers a stylish atmosphere with a menu of tapas and an excellent wine list. Enjoy dishes like lobster-stuffed squid and braised beef short ribs. Dinner here can cost between $40 and $60 per person. It is an ideal spot for a romantic dinner or a fun night out with friends.

Historic Sites and Places

The historic sites on the North Shore of Kauai offer a glimpse into the island's rich history and natural beauty.

- **Hanalei Pier:** Hanalei Pier is an iconic spot, originally built in the late 19th century to support the sugar industry. Today, it is a favorite for both locals and visitors. The pier provides stunning views of Hanalei Bay, and its calm waters are perfect for swimming and paddleboarding. It is a wonderful place to relax and soak in the serene beauty of the surroundings.

- **Waioli Mission House:** Step back in time at the Waioli Mission House, established in 1837 by early missionaries. This beautifully preserved house offers a look into the lives of those who first brought Christianity to the island. The mission house and its surrounding grounds are meticulously maintained, giving visitors a real sense of 19th-century Hawaiian life and the cultural exchanges that shaped the island.

- **Kilauea Lighthouse:** Perched on a dramatic cliff, the Kilauea Lighthouse, built in 1913, is a beacon of history and natural beauty. The lighthouse stands as a monument to maritime history and offers breathtaking views of the Pacific Ocean. The area is also a wildlife refuge, where you can spot seabirds and, if you are lucky, even humpback whales during the migration season.

- **Limahuli Garden and Preserve:** Limahuli Garden and Preserve is a living museum of Hawaiian flora. This botanical garden showcases native plants and traditional agricultural practices, nestled in a verdant valley against the backdrop of dramatic cliffs. It is an excellent spot to learn about the island's ecological and cultural history while enjoying its natural splendor.

- **Haena State Park:** Haena State Park is rich in natural beauty and cultural significance. Home to the ancient Ke'e Beach and the start of the famous Kalalau Trail, the park offers stunning landscapes, from lush forests to rugged coastlines. It is also a place of archaeological interest, with ancient Hawaiian sites such as the Haena Complex, including stone terraces and ceremonial platforms.

- **Napali Coast State Wilderness Park:** For the adventurous, Napali Coast State Wilderness Park is a must-visit. Accessible by hiking, boat, or helicopter, this park is famous for its towering sea cliffs, lush valleys, and remote beaches. The 11-mile Kalalau Trail offers a challenging hike with some of the most breathtaking scenery in Hawaii. Whether you are hiking, camping, or just taking in the views, the Napali Coast is an unforgettable experience.

In the next section, we will discuss fun activities that you can take part in on the Napali Coast. Stay tuned!

Chapter Seven

Hau'oli Nāpali Coast (Happy, Joyful, Cheerful)

I n this chapter, what follows is a perfect itinerary for the myriad adventures and activities you will find along this breathtaking coastline. Whether from an exciting boat tour, grand vistas from a lookout point, or viewing rugged beauty from the air in a helicopter, unforgettable landscapes await at Napali Coast. Find the attractions that surround it and plan an unforgettable trip to one of Hawaii's most iconic natural wonders.

Nāpali Coast Top Sights

The Na Pali Coast provides a wide range of awesome views and experiences that will leave one spellbound. Here are the top highlights.

- **Aerial Tours:** These are one of the most unforgettable experiences one can have aboard helicopters or small planes flying high above the Napali coastline. Sea cliffs, hidden valleys, and cascading waterfalls from the aerial tours along the coast offer special views of the features of the coast.

This is the best way to appreciate this fantastic natural wonder in full grandeur.

- **Boat Tours from Port Allen:** Departing from Port Allen, these boat tours get you really close to the rugged beauty of the coastline. You cruise past towering cliffs and may even pull into sea caves, possibly spotting dolphins and sea turtles. Most are combined with stops for snorkeling in the clear waters, part of the region's wide abundance of marine life.

- **Manawaiopuna Falls:** Most famous as the backdrop in the film "Jurassic Park," Manawaiopuna Falls is, without a doubt, an unforgettable sight. This majestic fall can only be accessed by a helicopter ride as you get into the cinematic experience of the powerful cascade down to a lush valley.

- **11-Mile Kalalau Trail:** The 11-Mile Kalalau Trail is a must for any hiking enthusiast. This was originally used by the Hawaiians of old, and it takes you along the coast, giving amazing views as well as access to private beaches. This trail terminates on the beautiful Kalalau Beach; allow yourself to camp amidst all the beauty that surrounds you.

- **Hanakapiai Beach:** Two miles into the trail of Kalalau, find this scenic spot that's perfect for a day hike. Through the forests and along the streams toward the ocean, the shoreline emerging is truly picturesque.

- **Milolii Valley:** is one of many hidden gems along the coast, accessible by boat or kayak. It's a place of absolute peace in which you can wander among ancient Hawaiian agricultural terraces in utter serenity.

- **Nualolo Kai and Nualolo Aina:** Both are archeological sites that show visitors a window to the life of the ancient Hawaiians. The Nualolo Kai and Nualolo Aina are accessible only by hiking tours. They both feature remains of traditional Hawaiian villages and terraces against stunning coastal backgrounds.

- **Kamaile:** Another beautiful place along the coast are the dramatic and awesome cliffs with panoramic views. The place is great for photography and ideal for just idling around while viewing your surroundings.

- **Open-Ceiling Cave:** A marvelous natural wonder, the product of a collapsed ceiling, and there is only one to be found. This is definitely one of those things where, in a boat tour, a person simply must see it, which holds a uniqueness that allows it to set a tone that feels out of this world.

- **Honopu:** This is separated from all beaches, surrounded by high cliffs, and is only accessible by swimming or boat. It has scenic views of a dramatic arch, and with its peaceful location, it is surely a favorite of adventurous travelers.

- **Kalalau Valley and Kalalau Beach:** This would be the epitome of everything Napali—the crown jewel. Cliffs with a rugged appearance surround the lush green carpet. At the brink of Kalalau Valley, discover Kalalau Beach. It is a sandy refuge like no other, which feels like paradise. Reaching it would make it a memorable destination by taking a hike along the Kalalau Trail or by boat.

Adventure Activities

During a journey on the Napali Coast, there are many adventure activities that assure you of the best experience in natural beauty.

Kayaking and Paddling on the Napali Coast

Visitors can take a kayak along the Napali Coast, exploring the towering cliffs and landing on hidden, secluded beaches. There are also guided kayak tours with plenty of historical and geological information about the area. Kayaking allows you to explore sea caves and other areas inaccessible by larger boats, making for a truly immersive adventure. Several tour operators offer guided kayak tours along the 17-mile stretch of the Napali Coast:

- **Napali Kayak** offers private guided tours and camping trips, allowing for a more intimate and personalized experience.

- **Kayak Kauai** provides open-ocean kayaking tours that take you through sea caves, pristine beaches, and areas rich in wildlife.

- **Bring Me a Kayak** rents out kayaks for self-guided exploration, perfect for those who prefer a more independent adventure.

- **Kayak Hanalei** departs from Hanalei Bay, giving easy access to the Napali Coast and its many wonders.

- **Ali'i Kayaks** offers rentals and guided tours, providing a comprehensive way to explore both the Napali Coast and other beautiful waterways of Kauai.

Snorkeling on the Napali Coast

Snorkeling along the Napali Coast reveals a vibrant underwater world teeming with marine life. Several tour operators offer diverse snorkeling experiences.

- **Captain J's Kauai Offshore Adventures** departs from the calmer, leeward waters of Kauai's southwest side, offering luxury super raft tours with excellent snorkeling opportunities along the 17-mile coastline.

- **Capt Andy's Kauai Snorkel Tours** provides steps into the water, all necessary gear, and expert snorkel instructions suitable for all levels. The friendly crew ensures a safe and enjoyable experience.

- **Blue Dolphin Charters** offers adventurous snorkel and scuba diving tours, including visits to the forbidden island of Niihau. Their tours include a variety of activities like swimming, snorkeling, floating on boogie boards, and even playing on a water slide.

Napali Coast State Wilderness Park: Hiking and Camping Opportunities

The Napali Coast is part of the Napali Coast State Wilderness Park, which offers incredible hiking and camping opportunities. However, permits are required for both activities.

- **Hours:** The park is open daily from 6:00 AM to 6:00 p.m.

- **Entrance Fee:** There is a nominal fee for entry, which helps maintain the park's facilities.

- **Trail Name:** The most famous trail is the 11-mile Kalalau Trail, renowned for its challenging terrain and stunning vistas.

- **Hiking Permits:** Required for day hiking beyond Hanakapiai Valley and can be obtained in advance.

- **Camping Permits:** Available 90 days in advance and necessary for overnight stays at Kalalau Beach.

- **Services and Facilities:** Basic amenities like composting toilets and designated camping areas are available.

- **Boat Transportation:** Some areas are accessible by boat, providing an alternative way to experience the coast.

- **Gear:** Essential gear includes sturdy hiking boots, camping equipment, and plenty of water.

Nearby Attractions to Nāpali Beach

The main attractions near the Napali Coast revolve around hiking, sightseeing, and water-based activities, allowing visitors to fully immerse themselves in the stunning natural beauty of this iconic Hawaiian landscape. Here's a glimpse of what you can expect at each nearby sight.

- **Kalalau Trail:** This strenuous 11-mile hiking trail is a highlight of the Napali Coast, offering adventurers dramatic coastal views, lush valleys, and access to secluded beaches. It's a challenging hike, but the rewards are worth every step.

- **Hanakapiai Falls:** Accessible from the Kalalau Trail, Hanakapiai Falls is a popular destination for hikers. The trail to the falls is about 4 miles round trip from Hanakapiai Beach, leading to a breathtaking 300-foot waterfall. It's a great spot for a refreshing dip after a hike.

- **Koke'e State Park:** Koke'e State Park features scenic lookout points and numerous hiking trails, many of which provide stunning views of the Napali Coast. The park is a fantastic spot for bird watching, exploring native flora, and taking in panoramic vistas.

- **Kokee Natural History Museum:** Located within Koke'e State Park, this museum offers fascinating insights into the natural and cultural history of the Napali region. It's an excellent stop for those interested in learning more about the area's unique ecosystem and heritage.

- **Ke'e Beach:** At the end of the road on Kauai's north shore lies Ke'e Beach, a picturesque spot known for its clear waters and excellent snorkeling. It also serves as the starting point for the Kalalau Trail, making it a popular gathering place for hikers.

- **Limahuli Garden and Preserve:** This botanical garden showcases native Hawaiian plants and offers educational tours with views of the Napali Coast. It's a peaceful retreat where you can learn about local plant species and conservation efforts.

- **Na Pali Catamaran Tours:** Experience the Napali Coast from the water with Na Pali Catamaran Tours. These boat tours provide a unique perspective of the coast's towering cliffs, sea caves, and marine life, offering an unforgettable adventure on the Pacific Ocean.

The next section is all about exploring Princeville. Flip the page to learn more!

Chapter Eight

The Prince of Kauai

Travel planning for Princeville is an exciting adventure. Princeville, an airy and opulent town with a view of the ocean and the honor of the entire Kauai island, is picturesque. This place comfortably nestles all the dreams of travelers: food lovers, outdoor lovers, or simply someone who would relish time on a calm holiday and walk around. The commercial town is vivid, with great local shops and first-class restaurants, scenic hikes, and water activities to make your turn a memorable one. Be prepared to learn all about the unique allure of Princeville and everything it has to offer you.

Princeville Top Sights

Let's have a look at the must-visit sights of Princeville.

- **Pu'u Poa or Pu'u Pa'oa:** The site of the Princeville Hotel, Pu'u Poa or Pu'u Pa'oa, holds significant cultural importance. "Pu'u" means mountain, and "Pa'ao" refers to the staff of the Fire Goddess Pele, who created new craters with her staff. Below the hotel lies Kamo'omaika'i, a marshy area that was once home to a large fishpond, reflecting the deep connection of the area to ancient Hawaiian traditions and natural beauty.

- **Buffalo Beach:** Buffalo Beach is a hidden gem in Princeville, offering a serene and less-crowded spot to enjoy the sun and sea. It is a great place for a quiet day by the water, whether you are sunbathing, swimming, or just enjoying the tranquil surroundings.

- **Makai Golf Course:** For golf enthusiasts, the Makai Golf Course is a must-visit. This beautifully designed course offers stunning ocean views and a challenging yet enjoyable round of golf. Whether you are a seasoned golfer or a beginner, the lush greens and dramatic landscapes make for an unforgettable golfing experience.

- **Sunset Circle:** Sunset Circle is the perfect spot to end your day in Princeville. As the name suggests, it offers breathtaking views of the sunset, making it a popular spot for visitors and locals alike. Bring a picnic, relax, and watch as the sky transforms into a canvas of vibrant colors.

- **Botanical Gardens and Chocolate Tasting:** Princeville is home to several botanical gardens that showcase the island's diverse flora. Many of these gardens also offer chocolate-tasting tours, where you can learn about and sample locally grown and produced chocolate. It is a delightful experience for both nature lovers and chocolate enthusiasts.

- **Shop at Princeville Center:** Princeville Center is the town's commercial hub, offering a variety of shops, restaurants, and services. From unique local boutiques to essential stores, you'll find everything you need. It is a great place to pick up souvenirs, enjoy a meal, or just stroll around and soak in the local atmosphere.

- **Princeville Night Market:** The Princeville Night Market is a vibrant event featuring local artisans, food vendors, live music, and more. Held monthly, it is a fantastic way to experience the local culture, shop for handmade goods, and enjoy delicious food in a lively setting.

- **Beaches in Princeville:** Princeville boasts several beautiful beaches, each offering a unique experience. Pali Ke Kua Beach, Puu Poa Beach, Wyllie Beach, and Secret Beach (Kauapea Beach) range from secluded, shady spots to open areas perfect for sunbathing. Whether you are looking for a peaceful retreat or a place to swim and snorkel, these beaches have something for everyone.

- **Hawaiian Luaus in Princeville:** A traditional Hawaiian luau is a must-do in Princeville, with costs typically ranging from $100 to $150 per person. These events immerse you in Hawaii's rich cultural heritage through Polynesian dance and music, delicious Hawaiian cuisine, and demonstrations of traditional arts like hula and lei-making. Participating in a luau offers a deeper appreciation of the island's traditions and is a memorable experience for all ages.

Adventure Activities in Princeville

Princeville is a great place for all nature lovers because there are several hiking and camping opportunities. The thick forests, huge cliffs, and many beautiful waterfalls along the lush trails are second to none. The camping opportunities in the nearby parks are plentiful; one is able to sleep under the stars and wake up with nature to feel totally cheerful. Do not forget to pack enough water, put on sturdy hiking boots, and check for any required permits before going out.

Ziplining

Feel the adrenaline pump through your veins as you fly through the air on a ziplining experience in Princeville. Count yourself high, high above the treetops, and appreciate a bird's-eye view of the awesome catalog of the island. Over three companies provide such thrills, which come in different lengths and difficulties so that both beginner and experienced thrill-seekers can enjoy them. Have the time of your life totally safe. Guides make sure all the equipment is properly on and everybody is secure.

ATV and 4WD trails

Have a wild off-road adventure in Princeville by taking an ATV or 4WD. The guided tours run across dirty paths, rocky roads, and deep into the wilderness of Kauai. Tickets range between $100 and $200 per guest and include safety gear and instructions to focus on the thrill of the ride.

Horseback Riding Tours

Experience the wild, great outdoors of Kauai on a horse in Princeville. Tour companies provide everything needed, including horses that will be able to accommodate guests at your skill level, as well as helmets. Nevertheless, for comfort and excellent safety, long pants and closed-toe shoes are required. Special consideration is taken for children, ensuring that they can have a safe and enjoyable time. Through lush valleys and scenic trials, you will feel in touch with the land in a most peaceful yet cheerful way.

Off-Road Trails

For those who like a bit of adventure, the off-road trails of Princeville lead over the island and into some of its most remote locations. The majority of the trails are only really accessible by foot, biking, or 4WD; they test the adventurous tourist through various landscapes of dense jungle and open fields with panoramic views, while the difficulty level can vary.

Bike Tours

Biking around Princeville is a great way to see the countryside at a leisurely pace. Guided bike tours provide a tour of local flora, fauna, and history along the way. Bike rentals are also available for those who would like to take the trail on their own. Make sure to wear a helmet and bring lots of water. Most people like the coastal routes, which offer fantastic views over the ocean and a refreshing breeze as you pedal your way through.

Nearby Attractions to Princeville

Here are some of the nearby attractions to Princeville that no one should miss.

Hideaways Beach (Pali Ke Kua Beach)

Hideaways Beach, also known as Pali Ke Kua Beach, is a hidden gem located beneath the cliffs of Princeville. With its golden sands and turquoise waters, it is the perfect spot for sunbathing, snorkeling, and enjoying the serene surroundings. Accessing this secluded beach involves a bit of a hike, but the stunning scenery and peaceful atmosphere make it well worth the effort.

Queen's Bath

Queen's Bath is a unique natural tide pool near the Princeville Resort. This spot is famous for its crystal-clear waters and fascinating marine life. However, it can be dangerous during high surf, so it is essential to check the weather and surf conditions before visiting. When it is safe, Queen's Bath offers a picturesque and tranquil place to explore and relax.

Hanalei Plantation Road Lookout

The Hanalei Plantation Road Lookout offers one of the best panoramic views in the area. From this scenic overlook, you can see the lush Hanalei River valley, the sparkling bay, and the pristine beaches stretching out before you. It is an excellent spot for photography or simply taking in the breathtaking landscape. Whether you are stopping by on your way to other adventures or spending a moment to soak in the view, this lookout is a must-visit.

The next chapter is all about planning your trip to Hanalei. Flip the page to learn more!

Thank You!

Share the Aloha Spirit with Your Review: Your Words Can Spark a Journey of Discovery

Our goal is to make every trip to Kauai an extraordinary one. But to do that, we need to reach out and touch the hearts of travelers everywhere.

By sharing your experience with The Kauai Travel and Adventure Guide, you're not just leaving a review. You're becoming a part of someone else's adventure, guiding them towards those hidden gems and unforgettable moments that you discovered. Mahalo!

Chapter Nine

The Beauty of Hanalei Bay

Nestled along Kauai's iconic North Shore lies the enchanting town of Hanalei, home to the pristine crescent of Hanalei Bay. This stretch of golden sand, embraced by lush, verdant mountains, is renowned for its postcard-perfect beauty and tranquil ambiance. Hanalei Bay beckons travelers to surrender to its timeless allure, where the rhythm of life slows to the gentle lull of rolling waves. This chapter will help you plan your trip to Hanalei, a place where you can unwind amidst nature's grandeur. Whether you are taking leisurely strolls along the palm-fringed shore, embarking on thrilling water adventures in crystal-clear waters, or basking in the warm glow of a Kauai sunset, Hanalei Bay promises an idyllic escape. Immerse yourself in the vibrant local culture of Hanalei town and discover why this coastal gem captivates the soul, leaving a lasting mark on every traveler.

Hanalei Bay

Hanalei Bay is the largest bay along the north shore of Kauai, Hawaii, stretching almost 2 miles and set before majestic mountains. In summer, it becomes a playground filled with sailboats, stand-up paddleboards, and swimmers, while in the winter, huge waves attract surfers to its breaks. Just beyond the bay is the small town of Hanalei, an idyllic old town that has boasted a rich history and agriculture. One of the historical landmarks in this little town is the Wai'oli Mission House, which is well-preserved to allow a peek into the missionary era of Hawaii and the original features of traditional Hawaiian architecture. Another important structure in the bay is the Hanalei Pier, located at the mouth of the Hanalei River. This historic structure is a very modern gathering place for fishing, picnicking, and swimming. It is often a favorite for families and offers a really stunning view of the bay and the mountains right around it.

The wetlands around Hanalei Bay were rich in agriculture, which was used for planting taro, a staple crop of the ancient Hawaiians. In the 1860s, the place was converted into rice farms, which prevailed for a very long time. A place where, even today, one can see fields of taro as part of landscape and culture. Hanalei Bay has also been the setting and backdrop for the movies "South Pacific" and "The Descendants," both of which did much to enhance its fabulous view on the silver screen. Hanalei is also a silver mine for anyone keen on improving their knowledge of traditional Hawaiian arts and crafts. There are many shops in Hanalei town where one can browse before buying handiwork produced for sale. Things that are produced for sale include tapestries, carved work in wood, and lauhala. The natural beauty and cultural traditions of Kauai are the inspiration for all of these. These galleries give the experience of getting special mementos—a representative of Hawaiian artistry.

Adventure Opportunities in Hanalei Bay

Adventure opportunities abound in Hanalei Bay, offering something for everyone, from snorkeling and surfing to stand-up paddleboarding.

Snorkeling

The waters around Hanalei Bay, including spots like Anini Beach and Hideaways, are perfect for snorkeling. Here, you can explore vibrant coral reefs teeming with tropical fish and other marine life. The area around Hanalei Pier also offers good snorkeling, with relatively calm waters and interesting underwater sights. Gear can be rented from local shops like Snorkel Bob's or Pedal 'n Paddle, but if you plan to snorkel frequently, investing in your own gear might be a good idea for a better fit and comfort.

Surfing

Hanalei Bay is a top surfing destination, especially in winter when the swells are larger. Always check the surf forecast before heading out to ensure safe and enjoyable conditions. For beginners and seasoned surfers alike, Hanalei offers something for everyone.

- **Ability Level:** Suitable for all levels; beginners can stick to the smaller waves near the pier, while advanced surfers can tackle the larger swells.

- **Local Vibe and Crowd Factor:** Friendly local surfers, but can get crowded, especially during peak seasons.

- **Water Quality and Hazards:** Generally good water quality, but always be mindful of potential hazards like rocks and coral.

- **Things to Bring:** Sunscreen, a rash guard, and a surfboard (rentals are available).

- **Access and Best Season:** Easily accessible with multiple entry points, the best surfing is in winter.

- **Rentals:** Surf shops in Hanalei, like Hanalei Surf School and Kauai Surf Rentals, offer lessons and board rentals, with lessons typically costing around $75-$100 for a two-hour session.

'Sup with that?—Stand-up Paddleboarding

Stand-up paddleboarding (SUP) in Hanalei Bay is a fantastic way to take in the stunning surroundings and tranquil waters. Several rental companies and tour operators, such as Hanalei River Watersports and Kayak Kauai, offer SUP rentals and guided tours. The calm, clear waters make Hanalei Bay an ideal location for SUP, providing a unique perspective of the lush landscapes and serene environment. Whether you are a beginner or an experienced paddler, SUP is an enjoyable way to explore Hanalei Bay's natural beauty.

With these activities, Hanalei Bay promises a memorable adventure for all types of water enthusiasts.

Photo Opportunities in Hanalei Bay

The historic Hanalei Pier is a must-see and provides fantastic photo opportunities, especially at sunrise or sunset. This iconic landmark stands out beautifully against the backdrop of the surrounding mountains and the expansive bay. Whether you are capturing the early morning light or the vibrant hues of a Hawaiian sunset, the pier adds a charming touch to your photos.

- **Scenic Landscapes:** Hanalei Bay is a photographer's dream with its stunning natural scenery. The crescent-shaped beach, lined with swaying palm trees and framed by lush green mountains, offers countless picturesque landscapes and seascapes. Every angle presents a new perspective, from the sweeping views of the bay to the intimate details of the coastal flora.

- **Water Activities:** The bay is a hub for water sports, providing ample opportunities for action shots. Snapping photos of people kayaking, stand-up paddleboarding, or surfing captures the dynamic energy of Hanalei Bay. These images not only highlight the adventurous spirit of the area but also showcase the beautiful, clear waters and vibrant activity that define the bay.

- **Aerial Perspectives:** For a unique perspective, consider aerial photography. Helicopter tours and drone photography can offer stunning bird's-eye views of Hanalei Bay and the Napali Coast beyond. These high-angle shots capture the grandeur of the landscape, from the winding coastline to the vast stretches of ocean and the dramatic cliffs that define the region.

- **Cultural Elements:** Hanalei is rich in cultural history, and places like the historic Waioli Mission provide interesting photographic subjects. These sites offer a glimpse into the island's past and its cultural heritage, adding depth and context to your photo collection. Capturing these elements can give your photos a narrative quality, telling the story of Hanalei's unique blend of natural beauty and cultural significance.

Hanalei Bay offers an abundance of photo opportunities that cater to both nature lovers and those interested in the island's rich cultural heritage. Whether you are taking wide-angle landscape shots, dynamic action photos, or intimate cultural images, Hanalei Bay has something to inspire every photographer.

Nearby Attractions

The areas surrounding Hanalei Bay offer a variety of natural, cultural, and recreational attractions for visitors to explore.

Waiʻoli (Pine Trees) Beach Park

This beach park is a local favorite, providing a great place to escape the heat with amenities like restrooms, outdoor showers, beach volleyball courts, and picnic tables. Known for its challenging shorebreak and big winter swells, it is particularly popular with local surfers. The mix of lush greenery and ocean views makes it a great spot for a relaxed afternoon.

Hanalei Pavilion Beach Park

Located along the crescent-shaped Hanalei Bay, Hanalei Pavilion Beach Park is perfect for swimming, walking, and taking in the scenic views. It is a great spot for families and visitors looking to enjoy the beach in a more leisurely fashion. The gentle waves and sandy shore make it ideal for a relaxing day by the water.

Waikoko Beach

Waikoko Beach, located on the western bend of Hanalei Bay, is known for its calmer waters and sandy bottom, offering safer swimming conditions compared to other parts of the bay. It is a great spot for those looking to enjoy a peaceful swim without the intensity of larger waves. The serene atmosphere and beautiful surroundings make it a perfect place for a quiet retreat.

Kilauea Point National Wildlife Refuge

A bit further afield, Kilauea Point National Wildlife Refuge is home to seabird nesting sites and the historic Kilauea Lighthouse, which stands at the northern-most point of the main Hawaiian islands. This area is a haven for bird watchers and nature enthusiasts, providing a unique opportunity to see native Hawaiian wildlife in a protected setting. The lighthouse itself is a picturesque landmark, offering stunning views of the ocean and rugged coastline.

Hanalei Bay is a must-visit for everyone coming to Kauai. In the next chapter, we will talk about Ha'ena State Park.

Chapter Ten

Ha'ena State Park Wonders

S ituated on Kauai's North Shore, Ha'ena State Park is a treasure trove of natural beauty and cultural significance. This chapter will guide you through planning an unforgettable visit to this stunning park. With its lush landscapes, ancient Hawaiian sites, and breathtaking coastal views, Ha'ena offers a mix of adventure and serenity. Whether you are hiking the famous Kalalau Trail, exploring the mystical sea caves, or simply basking in the sun on Ke'e Beach, Ha'ena State Park promises a memorable experience.

Ha'ena State Park

Ha'ena State Park, located at the northwestern end of Kuhio Highway on Kauai's north shore, is a destination that captivates with its rich natural beauty and historical significance. This park, often referred to as the "end of the road," marks the endpoint of Kuhio Highway and offers access to stunning beaches, scenic trails, and ancient Hawaiian sites. Among its most notable features are the sea caves, estimated to be over 4,000 years old, providing a fascinating glimpse into the island's past. One of the park's highlights is Ke'e Beach, a serene spot with a calm, reef-protected lagoon perfect for swimming and snorkeling. The beach's tranquil waters make it an ideal location for visitors looking to enjoy the ocean in a safe and relaxed environment. For those seeking adventure, Ha'ena State Park is also the trailhead for the famous 11-mile Kalalau Trail, which winds along the breathtaking Napali Coast. This trail is a must-do for avid hikers, offering challenging terrain and spectacular coastal views.

In addition to its natural attractions, Ha'ena State Park is steeped in cultural heritage. It is home to archaeological sites associated with hula, including a heiau (shrine) dedicated to Laka, the goddess of hula. These sites provide a unique opportunity to learn about the island's ancient traditions and make for intriguing photographic subjects. Due to its popularity, Ha'ena State Park has implemented daily visitor limits and requires advanced reservations for entry and parking. These measures were introduced following the park's closure for over a year after the 2018 floods, which allowed for the development of new management strategies. While Hawaii residents are exempt from the reservation and entry fee requirements, non-residents must purchase both entry and parking reservations prior to their visit.

Ha'ena State Park is also notable for its lush vegetation, particularly around Limahuli Stream, which enters the ocean at the eastern edge of the park. The area is surrounded by a variety of plants, including ironwood trees, coconut palms, ti plants, and guavas. The park's vegetation provides a beautiful backdrop for landscape and nature photography. The presence of native Hawaiian plant species, as well as some introduced species like strawberry guava, adds to the park's botanical diversity. The growth of sand dunes within the park is limited due to the presence of introduced tree stands, but the natural beauty remains unspoiled. Whether you are exploring the ancient sea caves, hiking the rugged trails, or simply enjoying the tranquil waters of Ke'e Beach, Ha'ena State Park offers a unique blend of natural splendor and cultural richness. This makes it a must-visit location for anyone looking to experience the essence of Kauai.

Adventure Activities Around Ha'Ena State Park

Ha'ena State Park is a treasure trove of adventure activities for outdoor enthusiasts. Located on Kauai's north shore, the park offers an array of experiences that cater to all kinds of adventurers, from hikers to beach lovers.

Hiking

Ha'ena State Park serves as the trailhead for the renowned Kalalau Trail, an 11-mile path that stretches along the breathtaking Napali Coast. This trail is not for the faint of heart; it presents a challenging and rewarding hike through some of the most stunning landscapes in Hawaii. The trail offers unparalleled views of the Pacific Ocean, rugged cliffs, and lush valleys. Hikers often feel a profound sense of accomplishment upon completing this demanding route. For those looking for a shorter adventure, the hike to Hanakapiai Beach and Falls is an excellent option. This trail is about 4 miles roundtrip from the park and offers a taste of the Napali Coast's beauty without the commitment of the full Kalalau Trail. The path winds through dense jungle, crosses the Hanakapiai Stream, and leads to a picturesque beach. Continuing another 2 miles inland brings you to the stunning Hanakapiai Falls, where you can take a refreshing dip in the pool beneath the waterfall.

Snorkeling and Swimming

Ke'e Beach, located within Ha'ena State Park, is a haven for snorkeling and swimming. The beach features a calm, reef-protected lagoon that makes it an ideal spot for these activities. The unique reef lagoon creates tranquil waters, perfect for exploring the underwater world without the challenge of strong currents. Snorkelers can expect to see a variety of tropical fish and possibly even sea turtles, making it a delightful experience for both novice and experienced snorkelers.

Beach Activities

Ke'e Beach is not only great for snorkeling and swimming but also offers a range of other beach activities. Visitors can enjoy shore fishing, where the tranquil waters and scenic surroundings provide a relaxing fishing experience. Sunbathing and picnicking are also popular activities, as the beach's soft sands and beautiful backdrop make it a perfect spot to unwind. Just east of Ha'ena State Park lies Ha'ena Beach, another excellent location for beach activities. This beach offers ample opportunities for sunbathing, swimming, and simply relaxing by the ocean. The views from Ha'ena Beach are spectacular, with the dramatic cliffs of the Napali Coast providing a stunning backdrop. It is a fantastic spot to soak up the sun, play in the sand, and enjoy the soothing sounds of the waves.

Exploring Ha'ena State Park and its surroundings provides a rich and varied adventure experience. Whether you are tackling the rigorous Kalalau Trail, marveling at the marine life while snorkeling at Ke'e Beach, or simply enjoying a leisurely day by the ocean, the park offers something for everyone. Its natural beauty, combined with the range of activities available, makes it a must-visit destination for anyone looking to experience the best of Kauai's outdoors. In the next section, we will discuss the east side of Kauai.

The Orient of Kauai

The area east of the island is commonly referred to as the "Coconut Coast" because of its high concentration of excitement and beauty mixed together. It makes this part of the island quite a stirring place for people who are into adventure and culture. This is the place of majestic waterfalls, with Wailua cascading gracefully amidst these verdant surroundings. The bustling town of Kapa'a offers a delightful mix of local shops, eateries, and galleries, providing a perfect spot to experience the island's charm and hospitality. Lihu'e is the historical capital of Kauai; tales of every nook and cranny depict the history of the island. From ancient heiau to maintained gardens, there is no shortage of ways to experience Kauai's history and natural beauty on the East Side. You can be assured of great memories in East Kauai, one of the most magical landscapes in Hawaii, whether on an exhilarating outdoor adventure or in a peaceful spot to reconnect with nature.

How to Get to the East Side of Kauai From Lihue Airport

When you arrive at Lihue Airport, you are already on the East Side of Kauai, making your journey to explore this beautiful region incredibly convenient. Located just a short distance from many of the island's key attractions, Lihue Airport is the perfect starting point for your adventure.

Driving Directions from Lihue Airport

From the airport, accessing the East Side of Kauai is straightforward and quick. Once you exit the airport, you will find yourself on the main highway, HI-56. This highway runs along the east coast of the island, connecting you to various destinations like Anahola, Kapaa, and Wailua in just about 15 minutes.

Proximity to East Side Attractions

Given its location, Lihue Airport serves as an ideal gateway to the East Side, often referred to as the Coconut Coast. As soon as you land, you are already in close proximity to some of Kauai's most popular spots. This part of the island is usually the first that visitors experience, providing a warm and scenic introduction to Kauai's charm.

Exploring the East Side

- **Anahola:** This quaint community is known for its beautiful beaches and relaxed vibe. A short drive north on HI-56 will lead you to Anahola Beach, perfect for swimming, picnicking, and enjoying the serene coastal views.

- **Kapaa:** Just a bit further north, Kapaa offers a blend of local culture and tourist-friendly amenities. Here, you can explore boutique shops, dine at local restaurants, and enjoy the Kapaa Bike Path, which offers stunning ocean views.

KAUAI TRAVEL AND ADVENTURE GUIDE COPY

- **Wailua:** South of Kapaa, Wailua is home to the majestic Wailua Falls and the sacred Wailua River. This area is rich in history and natural beauty, making it a must-visit on your tour of the East Side.

- **Coconut Coast:** Known for its swaying coconut palms and picturesque beaches, the Coconut Coast stretches along this eastern corridor, offering numerous spots for relaxation and adventure. Whether you are sunbathing on the beach, snorkeling in the clear waters, or exploring the local flora, the Coconut Coast encapsulates the essence of Kauai's natural allure.

Convenient Starting Point

Being located on the east side, Lihue Airport is inherently convenient for travelers looking to explore this part of the island. Its proximity to key attractions means you can start your adventure almost immediately after landing. The drive from the airport to the East Side destinations is short and scenic, with the main highway providing easy and direct access. Lihue Airport's location on Kauai's East Side makes it an excellent starting point for your island exploration. With a quick drive along HI-56, you will find yourself amidst the stunning scenery and vibrant culture of the East Side. From Anahola's tranquil beaches to Kapaa's lively streets and Wailua's historic sites, the East Side of Kauai offers a diverse and enchanting experience just a stone's throw from the airport.

Must-See Destinations

Exploring Kauai's East Side reveals a wealth of must-see destinations, each offering its own unique charm and attractions. From serene beach parks to scenic trails and cultural landmarks, here's a look at some of the top spots to visit.

Lydgate Beach Park

Situated in Lihue, Lydgate Beach Park is a gem for both locals and visitors. This beautiful beach setting is perfect for a variety of activities. The calm waters of the park's protected swimming areas make it an ideal spot for families with young children. You will find the Kamalani Playground here as well, a favorite for kids. There are also picnic tables and barbecue pits, making it a great spot for a beachside meal. The beach park is also known for its snorkeling opportunities, with abundant marine life just offshore.

Nounou-East Trail

For those who love hiking, the Nounou-East Trail in Kapa'a offers a rewarding experience. This moderate trail, often referred to as the Sleeping Giant Trail, provides hikers with stunning views of the island's lush landscape. As you ascend, you will pass through tropical forest areas and open ridges. The highlight of the hike is reaching the top of the Sleeping Giant, a prominent mountain ridge that offers panoramic views of Kauai. It is a great spot for photography and enjoying the natural beauty of the island.

Sleeping Giant East Trailhead

Starting from the Sleeping Giant East Trailhead in Kapa'a, hikers can embark on a journey to the summit of the Sleeping Giant. The trail is well-marked and offers several scenic overlooks along the way. The ascent is not too strenuous, making it accessible for most hikers. At the top, the views are breathtaking, encompassing the verdant valleys and sparkling coastline of Kauai. It is an ideal spot for a picnic or simply to rest and take in the scenery after the hike.

Kauai's Hindu Monastery

A visit to Kauai's Hindu Monastery in Kapa'a provides a unique cultural and spiritual experience. Set amidst lush tropical gardens, the monastery is a serene retreat that offers insight into Hindu practices and architecture. The grounds' serenity and beauty, which include a river, temple buildings, and meditation areas, frequently astound visitors. The monastery is open to the public for guided tours, where you can learn about the history and significance of this spiritual center. The intricate details of the temple and the peaceful environment make it a fascinating destination.

Each of these destinations on Kauai's East Side offers something special. Whether you are in the mood for a relaxing day at the beach, a hike with stunning views, or cultural exploration, there is something for everyone. The natural beauty and diverse attractions ensure that your visit to this part of the island will be memorable.

Where to Stay

Staying here would be the best area to stay on the island, not only because it is more convenient due to it being centrally located but also because it has some of the best accommodations on the island in all kinds of budgets or preferences for a stay. The east side contains a full range of choices for staying: hotels, resorts, and vacation rentals.

So let's start with perhaps the most luxurious of all: the **Kauai Beach Resort**. Located just miles away from Lihue Airport, the resort possesses a couple of pools and beautifully landscaped grounds with beach access. With a modern resort room at the place having just ranged between $200 and $400 a night, it would likely be the perfect place for anyone interested in all the comfort and a lot of convenience.

Hilton Garden Inn Kauai Wailua Bay is a mid-range option that will get you near the river and offers a quite comfortable stay with somewhat contemporary amenities. Prices are around $150–$250 per night. It perfectly suits the interests of couples or families who want to stay near the beach and close to the Fern Grotto and Wailua Falls.

Budget travelers are going to feel like they have hit the jackpot with a stay at the **Kauai Shores Hotel**. This vibrantly decorated, colorful hotel is found right on the beach in Kapa'a, complete with a pool and just an easygoing feel. The cost of a room usually ranges from $100 to $200 per night, making it ideal for anybody desiring to experience the beauty of Kauai without spending a fortune.

For those who want a more home-like experience, there's the **Aston Islander on the Beach**. Along the Coconut Coast, one more property offers its guest condo-style rooms with kitchenettes, making it perfect for more consecutive stays. The place also features tropical gardens and sits on the beachfront. These units usually range in price from $150 to $250, giving travelers a nice balance between quality and affordability.

Another great mid-range hotel is the **Courtyard by Marriott Kauai** at Coconut Beach. This beachfront property is very modern in terms of style and contains large rooms and a full-service spa. Moreover, the pool area is really welcoming. The pricing usually stays between $200 and $300 per night, which is really nice for any kind of traveler who likes to kick back and relax.

For those guests who prefer vacation rentals, Kapa'a has **Kreller's Getaway,** which has a number of condos that can accommodate different numbers of guests according to the size of the condo. They will usually include an equipped kitchen and private lanai, which would give you that sense of a home away from home. Most will allow you to rent per night, typically from $100 to $250, according to size and according to season.

For something completely different and peaceful, there is the **Fern Grotto Inn**. The cute-as-a-button property has the charm of a cluster of renovated plantation cottages near the banks of the Wailua River. The individually designed cottages offer a quiet oasis from the hustle and bustle found everywhere else. Rates tend to run $150 to $300 nightly in this one-of-a-kind bit of history and comfort.

Staying on the east side of Kauai puts you within easy reach of the island's most beautiful beaches, sea cliffs, and hikes—all within easy reach of all parts of the island; it is a great home base for your Kauai adventure. With that kind of variety in accommodations, from the cheapest to the style-motivated, the east side does have something for everyone.

Popular Beaches on the East Side of Kauai

Exploring the east side of Kauai is a beach lover's paradise. This area is home to some of the most beautiful and accessible beaches on the island, each offering unique experiences. Whether you are looking to relax, swim, or snorkel, there is a beach for you on Kauai's east side.

Lydgate Beach Park is a family favorite and one of the safest beaches on the island. The park features a large, protected swimming area perfect for children and inexperienced swimmers. The enclosed lagoon is filled with colorful fish, making it an excellent spot for snorkeling. The park also offers picnic tables, playgrounds, and ample parking, making it a convenient spot for a day out with the family.

Keālia Beach is another popular destination, particularly for surfers and boogie boarders. With its long stretch of golden sand and strong waves, it is a fantastic spot for those looking to catch some surf. There is also a lifeguard on duty, which adds an extra layer of safety for swimmers. If you are not into surfing, it is a great beach for sunbathing or taking long walks along the shore.

For those seeking a quieter, more secluded experience, **Donkey Beach** is a hidden gem. Located just north of Keālia Beach, it is a bit of a hike to get there, but the effort is well worth it. The beach is less crowded, offering a peaceful retreat where you can relax and enjoy the natural beauty of Kauai. The waves can be rough, so it is not ideal for swimming, but it is perfect for sunbathing and picnicking.

Anahola Beach is another fantastic option, especially for families. The beach is located within Anahola Bay, which provides calm waters perfect for swimming and snorkeling. The sandy bottom and clear waters make it a great spot for kids to splash around safely. The beach also offers amenities like picnic tables, restrooms, and ample shade from the coconut palm.

Wailua Beach is located near the mouth of the Wailua River and is a popular spot for both locals and visitors. The beach offers a mix of golden sand and scenic views, with the lush mountains in the background. It is a great place for a morning jog or a sunset walk. The waves here can be strong, making it a favorite for surfers and bodyboarders, but swimming can be a bit challenging.

Kapa'a Beach Park is centrally located and a great spot for a quick dip or a picnic. The park has a grassy area perfect for lounging, as well as a playground for kids.

The beach itself is small but charming, and the shallow waters are safe for wading. It is also conveniently located near shops and restaurants, making it easy to grab a bite to eat after a day at the beach.

Fuji Beach, also known as Baby Beach, is ideal for families with young children. The shallow, protected waters create a natural wading pool where little ones can safely play. The beach is named for its proximity to the historic Fuji House and is a great spot for a relaxed, low-key beach day. Each beach on Kauai's east side offers something unique, from the tranquil waters of Anahola Beach to the surf-friendly waves of Keālia Beach. No matter what kind of beach experience you are looking for, you will find it along the Coconut Coast, where the beauty of Kauai is always on display.

The next chapter is all about exploring Lihu'e. So, stay tuned to learn more!

Chapter Twelve

The Capital Town of Lihu'e

V isiting the town of Lihu'e should not be just about passing through the airport. As the capital town of Kauai, Lihu'e has a lot to offer that makes it worth exploring. From historical sites to local eateries, this charming town is packed with hidden gems that can enrich your Kauai experience. Located on the southeastern coast of the island, Lihu'e is the perfect blend of convenience and culture. It is home to the island's main airport, but there is so much more to discover beyond the terminals. If you are a history buff, the Kauai Museum offers fascinating insights into the island's past, showcasing artifacts from ancient Hawaiian culture to the plantation era.

For outdoor enthusiasts, Nawiliwili Harbor and Kalapaki Beach provide stunning coastal views and a range of activities, from paddleboarding to beach volleyball. And if you are interested in local cuisine, the town's farmers markets are brimming with fresh produce and homemade goodies, giving you a true taste of Kauai. Lihu'e is also a great starting point for exploring other parts of the island, thanks to its central location. Whether you are heading north to the scenic Hanalei Bay or south to the sunny shores of Poipu, Lihu'e serves as a convenient hub. So, next time you are in town, take a moment to explore and enjoy what Lihu'e has to offer.

About Lihu'e Town

Lihu'e, the second-largest town on the Hawaiian island of Kauai, holds a unique blend of history, culture, and natural beauty. Named "cold chill" in Hawaiian, Lihu'e is nestled in the ancient district of Puna on the southeastern coast of the island, within the ahupua'a of Kalapaki. Lihu'e is an essential hub on Kauai, bustling with activity and providing vital services to both residents and visitors. The town's geography is characterized by its scenic coastal views and lush land-scapes, making it a picturesque destination. With a population of around 6,500 people, Lihu'e offers a small-town feel with the amenities of a larger community.

Transportation

Getting around Lihu'e is straightforward. The town is home to Kauai's main airport, Lihue Airport (LIH), making it the primary entry point for visitors to the island. Public transportation is available, but renting a car is recommended for more flexibility in exploring the area.

Facilities

Lihu'e boasts a variety of facilities, including shopping centers, medical services, and government offices. Kukui Grove Shopping Center is a popular spot for retail therapy, and the town also hosts several farmer's markets where you can find fresh local produce.

History of Lihu'e

The town's history is deeply intertwined with the sugar industry, which took root in the 1800s. Lihu'e rose to prominence with the construction of a large sugar mill, marking its transformation into the island's central city. Early investors like Henry A. Peirce, Charles Reed Bishop, and William Little Lee played crucial roles in its development. William Harrison Rice created the first irrigation system in 1856, which helped the struggling plantation prosper. Paul Isenberg, a subsequent plantation owner, facilitated the emigration of German settlers to Lihu'e in 1881, leading to the establishment of Hawaii's first Lutheran church in 1883. By the 1930s, George Norton Wilcox had become one of the largest sugarcane plantation owners on the island. His acquisition of Grove Farm from Hermann A. Widemann and the conversion of the Wilcox family home, Kilohana, into a restaurant and gift shop are notable historical landmarks.

How to Get to Lihu'e

Reaching Lihu'e is convenient via Lihue Airport, which is well-connected with direct flights from various mainland cities. From the airport, you can easily access the town by rental car, shuttle, or taxi.

Food Tours

Lihu'e offers a delightful culinary scene with food tours that allow you to sample local delicacies. From fresh seafood to traditional Hawaiian dishes, the town's eateries cater to diverse tastes. Be sure to check out local favorites and farmer's markets for an authentic taste of Kauai.

Places to See

* **Downtown Lihu'e:** Downtown Lihu'e is a vibrant area with shops, restaurants, and historical sites. Stroll through the town to experience its unique blend of modern amenities and historical charm.

* **Kilohana Estate,** once the home of the Wilcox family, is now a restaurant and gift shop surrounded by lush plantations that are growing various crops and livestock. It is a great spot to enjoy a meal and learn about the island's agricultural history.

* **Kauai Museum:** The Kauai Museum offers fascinating exhibits on the island's history and culture, providing a deep dive into its rich heritage.

- **Kalapaki Beach:** Kalapaki Beach is perfect for relaxing and enjoying water activities like swimming and paddleboarding. Its beautiful crescent shape and calm waters make it a favorite among locals and visitors alike.

- **Kauai Humane Society:** Animal lovers should visit the Kauai Humane Society, where you can meet adoptable pets or take a shelter dog on a field trip for the day.

- **Ninini Point Lighthouse:** For stunning views, head to Ninini Point Lighthouse. This historic lighthouse offers panoramic vistas of the coastline and the ocean.

- **Alakoko Fishpond:** The ancient Alakoko Fishpond, also known as Menehune Fishpond, is a fascinating site that showcases early Hawaiian aquaculture ingenuity.

- **Grove Farm Homestead Museum:** Explore the Grove Farm Homestead Museum to get a glimpse of life on a historic sugar plantation, complete with well-preserved buildings and artifacts.

- **Koloa Rum Company:** End your visit with a tour of the Koloa Rum Company, where you can learn about rum production and enjoy tastings of locally-made rums.

Places to Stay in Lihu'e Town

Lihu'e offers a range of accommodations to suit any budget, making it a great base for exploring Kauai. Here are seven places to consider for your stay in Lihu'e.

- **Kauai Palms Hotel:** For those seeking budget-friendly accommodations, Kauai Palms Hotel is a fantastic choice. Located close to the airport and downtown Lihu'e, this hotel offers clean and comfortable rooms without breaking the bank. Prices typically range from $100 to $150 per night. It is perfect for travelers who want convenience and affordability.

- **Tip Top Motel:** Another budget-friendly option is Tip Top Motel. Famous for its on-site restaurant serving local favorites, this motel provides basic yet comfortable rooms. With rates around $100 per night, it is a great spot for budget-conscious travelers looking to stay in the heart of Lihu'e.

- **Banyan Harbor Resort:** Mid-range travelers will appreciate Banyan Harbor Resort. Located near Kalapaki Beach, this resort offers spacious condo-style accommodations with full kitchens. Prices range from $150 to $250 per night. It is ideal for families or those planning a longer stay, as the extra space and amenities add convenience.

- **Kauai Inn:** Set in a lush, garden-like setting, the Kauai Inn is a charming mid-range option. It offers a relaxing atmosphere, with rooms priced between $150 and $200 per night. The inn's historic significance and warm hospitality make it a delightful place to stay.

- **Marriott's Kauai Lagoons:** For a more upscale experience, Marriott's Kauai Lagoons provides luxurious villa accommodations. With stunning ocean views, golf courses, and top-notch amenities, prices here range from $300 to $500 per night. It is perfect for those seeking a premium stay with all the comforts of home.

- **Royal Sonesta Kauai Resort:** Located on Kalapaki Beach, the Royal Sonesta Kauai Resort offers a premium experience with its beautiful beachfront setting, multiple dining options, and a full-service spa. Nightly rates start around $350 and can go up depending on the season and room type. It is ideal for travelers looking to indulge in luxury.

- **Timbers Kauai Ocean Club & Residences:** For the ultimate luxury experience, Timbers Kauai offers high-end residences with breathtaking ocean views, private pools, and personalized service. Rates typically start at $600 per night. This is the place for those wanting an exclusive and luxurious retreat.

Places to Eat

Lihu'e has a vibrant food scene with a range of options to satisfy every palate and budget. Here are seven fantastic places to eat in Lihu'e Town, ranging from budget-friendly to premium dining experiences.

- **Duke's Kauai:** Located on Kalapaki Beach, Duke's Kauai is a must-visit for its relaxed beachfront vibe and delicious food. Enjoy fresh seafood, steaks, and tropical cocktails while soaking in the stunning ocean views. It is mid-range in price, with entrees typically ranging from $20 to $40.

- **Hualani's:** For a more upscale dining experience, head to Hualani's at the Timbers Kauai resort. This farm-to-table restaurant offers gourmet dishes made with locally sourced ingredients. The elegant atmosphere and exquisite cuisine make it perfect for a special night out. Expect to spend $50 to $100 per person.

- **Lilikoi Bar and Grill:** Lilikoi Bar and Grill is a local favorite for its casual atmosphere and delicious menu featuring American and Hawaiian dishes. Located in the heart of Lihu'e, it is a great spot for lunch or dinner with family and friends. Prices are moderate, with most dishes ranging from $15 to $30.

- **Cafe Portofino:** If you are in the mood for Italian, Cafe Portofino offers a fine dining experience with an oceanfront view. Enjoy a wide selection of wines while dining on traditional Italian dishes like pasta, risotto, and fresh seafood. Entrees typically cost between $25 and $50, making it a great choice for a romantic evening.

- **Noka Grill:** Noka Grill is a hidden gem offering a mix of Asian and American cuisine. This casual eatery is known for its friendly service and tasty dishes like poke bowls, burgers, and grilled fish. It is budget-friendly, with most items priced under $15, making it a perfect spot for a quick, satisfying meal.

- **Konohiki Seafoods:** For the freshest seafood in town, head to Konohiki

Seafoods. This local favorite offers a variety of poke, sashimi, and other seafood dishes at reasonable prices. It is a great place to grab a delicious, budget-friendly meal, with prices generally ranging from $10 to $20.

- **Mariachi's Mexican Cuisine:** Mariachi's Mexican Cuisine brings a taste of Mexico to Lihu'e with its vibrant flavors and festive atmosphere. Enjoy classic Mexican dishes like tacos, enchiladas, and fajitas, all made with fresh ingredients. It is a mid-range option, with most entrees costing between $12 and $25.

In the next section, we will explore the Wailua Falls. Are you ready for a new adventure?

Chapter Thirteen

Finding Your Pu'Uhonua in Wailua (Place of Refuge; Sanctuary; Safe Haven)

Discovering a place of refuge in Wailua is more than just a visit; it is an invitation to connect with the serene beauty and cultural richness of Kauai. Wailua, often referred to as a sanctuary, offers a tranquil escape from the hustle and bustle, allowing you to find your own pu'uhonua or place of refuge. One of the highlights of Wailua is the breathtaking Wailua Falls. This stunning double waterfall, cascading over 80 feet into a lush, tropical pool, is a must-see for anyone visiting Kauai. The falls are not only a visual delight but also hold cultural significance; they are believed to be a bathing site for Hawaiian royalty.

Planning a visit to Wailua Falls can be an enriching experience. Early in the morning is the best time to catch the falls in their full glory, as the sunlight creates beautiful rainbows in the mist. The falls are easily accessible by car, and there is a viewpoint just a short walk from the parking area, providing a perfect spot for photographs and quiet contemplation. In addition to the falls, Wailua is home to several other natural and cultural attractions, making it an ideal destination for those seeking both adventure and peace. Whether you are hiking along the trails, exploring the historic sites, or simply relaxing by the falls, Wailua offers a sanctuary where you can reconnect with nature and yourself.

Wailua Falls

Wailua Falls, located just north of Lihue at the southern end of the Wailua River, is one of Kauai's most captivating natural attractions. This stunning double-tiered waterfall is incredibly accessible, making it a perfect spot for all visitors. You can drive right up to the parking lot, which offers a fantastic view of the falls without any need for hiking. Physically, Wailua Falls is a spectacle to behold. It plunges dramatically, between 80 and 200 feet, depending on rainfall, into a beautiful pool below. The exact height of the falls can vary, and after heavy rains, the falls are particularly impressive, with water thundering down in a powerful display. The falls split into two streams as they cascaded down, creating a picturesque and iconic image.

Known for its breathtaking beauty, Wailua Falls has garnered significant popularity and notoriety over the years. It achieved a kind of celebrity status when it was featured in the opening credits of the classic TV show "Fantasy Island." This exposure has made it one of Kauai's most famous landmarks. Its natural charm, combined with the ease of access, makes it a must-see for anyone visiting the island. While Wailua Falls is a beautiful and accessible spot, it is important to heed safety warnings. The allure of hiking down to the base of the falls is strong for many adventurers, but it is highly discouraged. The descent is steep, slippery, and treacherous, and numerous accidents and fatalities have occurred over the years. The county has placed clear warning signs to dissuade visitors from attempting the dangerous hike. For your safety, it is best to enjoy the view from the designated overlook.

In addition to the falls themselves, the surrounding area offers plenty to explore. The Wailua River is the only navigable river in Hawaii, providing opportunities for kayaking and boat tours. Nearby, you can find other attractions, such as the Wailua River State Park, which houses the Fern Grotto, and the Wailua Complex of Heiaus, ancient Hawaiian places of worship. The beauty and tranquility of Wailua Falls make it a perfect spot for reflection and appreciation of nature's grandeur. Whether you are a photography enthusiast looking to capture the perfect shot, a nature lover eager to soak in the scenery, or simply a traveler seeking a peaceful moment amidst your adventures, Wailua Falls is a destination that won't disappoint.

Wailua Falls stands out not just for its stunning visual appeal but also for its accessibility and historical significance. While it is a safe and straightforward stop for most travelers, always remember to respect nature's power and the safety guidelines in place. Enjoy the majestic sight of the falls from the overlook, take in the surrounding natural beauty, and let the tranquility of this incredible spot enrich your visit to Kauai.

Adventure Activities at Wailua Falls

Experiencing Wailua Falls is an adventure lover's dream, with several exciting activities offering different perspectives of this magnificent natural wonder.

Helicopter Tours

If you are looking for a thrilling way to see Wailua Falls, helicopter tours are a fantastic option. These tours provide breathtaking panoramic views from above, showcasing the cascading waterfalls in all their glory. From the air, you will also get a bird's-eye view of the lush, verdant landscapes that surround the falls. It is an exhilarating experience that offers unparalleled photo opportunities and a new appreciation for the scale and beauty of Kauai's terrain.

Kayaking Tours

For those who prefer an adventure on the water, kayaking tours to Wailua Falls are a popular choice. Paddling along the Wailua River, you will immerse yourself in a serene and scenic environment that can only be fully appreciated at a leisurely pace. The kayak journey offers a unique perspective of the falls and allows for exploration of the river's diverse ecosystems. Along the way, you might spot native birds, tropical flora, and perhaps even a glimpse of wildlife. These tours often include knowledgeable guides who share fascinating insights about the history and natural features of the area.

Hiking Adventures

Hiking to Wailua Falls is a fantastic way to engage directly with the natural surroundings and get up close to the majestic cascades. However, it is important to note that while the falls can be admired from an easily accessible overlook, hiking down to the base is both challenging and risky. This hike is not officially sanctioned due to safety concerns, but for the adventurous, here's what you need to know.

- **Elevation Gain and Difficulty:** The hike involves a steep descent with significant elevation change. The trail is rugged, muddy, and can be very slippery, especially after rainfall. It is considered difficult and is only recommended for experienced hikers with a good fitness level.

- **Trailhead:** The informal trailhead is near the parking lot, but it is not well-marked. Locals sometimes provide guidance, but be prepared for a lack of clear signage.

- **What to Bring:** Wear sturdy hiking boots with good traction. A walking stick can help with balance on the slippery slopes. Bring plenty of water, as the tropical climate can be very humid. Bug spray and sunscreen are also essential.

- **Safety Tips:** This hike can be dangerous. The county has posted signs advising against it due to past injuries and fatalities. If you decide to go, proceed with extreme caution. Always check weather conditions beforehand, as the trail becomes even more hazardous when wet.

Exploring Wailua Falls through these adventurous activities allows for a deeper connection with Kauai's natural beauty. Whether soaring above in a helicopter, paddling on a tranquil river, or embarking on a challenging hike, each experience offers a unique and memorable way to witness the splendor of this iconic water-fall. Always prioritize safety and respect local guidelines to ensure your adventure is both thrilling and safe.

Photo Opportunities

Exploring the Wailua Falls Trail is not only an adventure but also a paradise for photography enthusiasts. The trail offers an array of opportunities to capture the natural beauty and thrill of the hike. Here are some prime spots for taking memorable photos.

Scenic Views

The hike is abundant with scenic views that showcase the lush surroundings. As you trek through dense vegetation and navigate rugged terrain, you will find numerous vantage points to snap stunning landscape photos. The backdrop of verdant foliage, combined with glimpses of the waterfall, creates breathtaking compositions that highlight the beauty of Kauai's natural environment.

Waterfall Shots

One of the highlights of the hike is photographing Wailua Falls. This majestic triple-flow waterfall can be captured from various angles along the trail. The sight of the cascading water is truly mesmerizing, whether you are photographing it from a distance, with the jungle as a backdrop, or closer up. Early morning or late afternoon light can add a magical glow to your shots, enhancing the waterfall's natural splendor.

Action Shots

The trail's muddy and somewhat steep descent is perfect for action shots. Capture hikers navigating the tricky terrain, using ropes for support, or simply embracing the adventure. These dynamic photos convey the trail's challenging and exhila-rating nature, making for compelling and lively images.

Close-up Details

Do not miss the opportunity to capture close-up details of the flora and fauna along the trail. Photos of unique plants, intricate root systems, and the textures of rocks can add depth to your photographic narrative. These shots highlight the smaller, often overlooked elements that make the Wailua Falls Trail so special.

The Base of the Falls

Reaching the base of Wailua Falls offers a unique perspective that is perfect for photography. Here, you can capture the waterfall's raw power and beauty up close. Shots from this vantage point emphasize the sheer force and elegance of the water as it cascades down, creating misty, dramatic images that are sure to impress.

Photographing the Wailua Falls Trail is an exciting way to document your adventure while showcasing the diverse beauty of Kauai's landscapes. From sweeping scenic views to intimate close-ups, each photo opportunity adds to the rich tapestry of your hiking experience. In the next section, we will discuss the charming towns of East-side Kauai, Kapa'a.

Chapter Fourteen

Kapa'a-ing Along the Coconut Coast

Nestled along the Coconut Coast, Kapa'a is one of the most charming towns on Kauai's east side. This chapter will help you plan an unforgettable visit to this vibrant destination, known for its laid-back vibe, rich culture, and stunning scenery. Kapa'a is a treasure trove of unique shops, delicious eateries, and local art galleries. As you stroll through the town, you will discover an eclectic mix of boutiques and markets offering everything from handcrafted jewelry to Hawaiian quilts. Foodies will delight in the array of dining options, from food trucks serving up local favorites to cozy cafes and beachfront restaurants.

Outdoor enthusiasts will find plenty to do in and around Kapa'a. The town is a gateway to some of the island's best hiking and biking trails, including the scenic Ke Ala Hele Makalae coastal path. The nearby beaches offer fantastic opportunities for swimming, snorkeling, and paddleboarding. In Kapa'a, the spirit of aloha is alive and well. Whether you are exploring the historic landmarks, enjoying the natural beauty, or simply soaking in the relaxed island atmosphere, this delightful town promises a memorable experience. Get ready to immerse yourself in the charm and hospitality that make Kapa'a a must-visit on your Kauai adventure.

KAUAI TRAVEL AND ADVENTURE GUIDE COPY

Kapa'a Town: Kauai's Most Charming Town

Nestled on the east side of Kauai, just north of Lihue, lies the charming town of Kapa'a. With a population of around 10,000, Kapa'a offers a delightful blend of small-town charm and vibrant culture, making it a must-visit destination for anyone exploring Kauai.

Attractions and Activities

Kapa'a is a popular tourist spot, brimming with hotels, condos, restaurants, and shops. One of its most iconic features is the Sleeping Giant mountain formation, visible from various points around the town. Outdoor enthusiasts will love the Ke Ala Hele Makalae, a scenic 9-mile coastal path perfect for walking and biking that runs right through Kapa'a, offering stunning ocean views and a great way to experience the island's natural beauty.

The town is also home to a vibrant weekly farmers market, where you can find fresh local produce, handcrafted goods, and a taste of the island's culinary delights. On the first Saturday of each month, Kapa'a hosts an art walk, showcasing the talents of local artists and providing a festive atmosphere with live music and food vendors.

History and Culture

Kapa'a has a rich and diverse history. The area was originally inhabited by ancient Hawaiians, who relied on reef fishing and agriculture. In the late 1800s, the establishment of the Makee Sugar Company brought an influx of workers from China, Portugal, Japan, and the Philippines, contributing to the town's cultural mosaic. This diverse heritage is reflected in Kapa'a's historic downtown area, where many buildings from this era still stand, providing a glimpse into the town's past.

Transportation and Challenges

While Kapaʻa is known for its quaint charm, it is also notorious for heavy traffic during rush hours. However, the implementation of a bypass road and contra-flow hours has helped alleviate some of the congestion, making it easier for visitors and locals alike to navigate the town.

Kapaʻa Murals

Kapaʻa is also known for its vibrant murals, which adorn various buildings around town. These murals reflect the town's cultural heritage, natural beauty, and artistic spirit, making for excellent photo opportunities and adding a splash of color to your visit.

Business of Old Kapaʻa Town

The businesses in old Kapaʻa town have a distinct character and are often family-owned and operated, providing a personal touch that larger commercial areas lack. These shops range from antique stores to local boutiques, offering unique souvenirs and a taste of authentic Kauai.

Places to See

- **Lydgate Farms:** This beautiful farm offers tours where you can learn about the cultivation of cacao and taste delicious chocolates made on-site.

- **Hoʻolalaea Waterfall:** A stunning waterfall that is easily accessible and provides a perfect backdrop for photos.

- **Lae Nani Beach:** Known for its serene atmosphere, this beach is ideal for a relaxing day by the ocean.

- **Hindu Monastery and Kadavul Hindu Temple:** These spiritual sites offer a serene environment for reflection and are architecturally stunning.

- **St. Catherine of Alexandria Parish:** is a historic church that is worth visiting for its beautiful architecture and peaceful ambiance.

- **Crossroads Christian Fellowship:** is a welcoming community where you can attend services and engage with locals.

- **The Glass Shack:** is a unique shop where you can find beautiful glass art created by local artisans.

Must-See Destinations

- **Lydgate Beach Park:** Located in Lihue, Lydgate Beach Park offers a beautiful beach setting. It is a popular spot for swimming, picnicking, and enjoying the ocean views.

- **Nounou-East Trail:** The Nounou-East Trail in Kapa'a offers a moderate hiking experience with beautiful views. The trail leads to the Sleeping Giant, a prominent mountain ridge on the island.

- **Sleeping Giant East Trailhead:** The Sleeping Giant East Trailhead in Kapa'a offers a scenic hiking experience. Visitors can enjoy panoramic views of the area from the trail.

- **Kauai's Hindu Monastery:** Kauai's Hindu Monastery in Kapa'a provides a unique cultural and spiritual experience. It offers insights into Hindu practices and architecture.

Dining and Shopping

Kapa'a boasts a variety of dining options, from food trucks serving local Hawaiian cuisine to fine dining establishments offering international flavors. The town's shopping scene is equally diverse, with numerous boutiques, craft shops, and markets where you can find everything from locally made jewelry to traditional Hawaiian clothing.

- **Java Kai:** is a popular coffee shop in Kapa'a known for its excellent coffee and delicious breakfast options.

- **Pono Market:** A great place to sample local Hawaiian dishes, Pono Market is a must-visit for food enthusiasts.

Festivals and Events

Kapa'a is home to several annual festivals and events that celebrate the local culture and community. These include the Coconut Festival, which highlights the many uses of coconut, and the Kapa'a Music and Art Festival, featuring local musicians and artists.

Kapa'a is more than just a stop on your Kauai itinerary; it is a destination that captures the heart with its mix of natural beauty, cultural richness, and warm hospitality. Whether you are exploring its historic sites, enjoying the scenic coastal path, or immersing yourself in local events, Kapa'a offers a unique and unforgettable experience on the Garden Isle.

Adventure Activities at Kapa'a

Kapa'a offers an array of adventure activities for outdoor enthusiasts. Whether you prefer biking along scenic coastal paths, engaging in thrilling water sports, or exploring lush trails on foot or horseback, Kapa'a has something for everyone.

Biking

One of the best ways to experience Kapa'a is by biking along the Ke Ala Hele Makalae coastal bike path. This picturesque route offers breathtaking ocean views and a scenic ride from Lydgate Park to Donkey Beach. It's a perfect way to soak in the natural beauty of Kauai at a leisurely pace. For bike rentals, Hele on

Kauai provides a range of options, making it easy for visitors to hop on and start exploring.

Water Sports

Kapa'a is a haven for water sports enthusiasts. Whether you are into water skiing or kayaking, there are plenty of opportunities for fun and adventure on the water. Kayak rentals are readily available, allowing you to paddle through the serene waters of the Wailua River or explore the coastal areas. The thrill of gliding over the water while taking in the stunning surroundings is an experience not to be missed.

Hiking

For those who prefer exploring on foot, Kapa'a offers several hiking trails that showcase the island's natural beauty. The Kauai Path, a network of trails, provides easy access to various scenic spots. The Sleeping Giant Trail (Nounou Mountain Trail) is a favorite, offering a moderate hike with rewarding views from the summit. For a more challenging trek, the Kuilau Ridge Trail and Makaleha Falls Trail promise lush landscapes and stunning vistas. The Moalepe Trail is another excellent option, known for its peaceful setting and panoramic views.

Golfing

If golf is your game, do not miss the opportunity to play a round at the Wailua Golf Course. This course is renowned for its challenging layout and welcoming atmosphere, providing a fun and active outdoor experience. With stunning views and well-maintained greens, it is a great way to spend a leisurely day in Kapa'a.

Horseback Riding

For a unique adventure, consider horseback riding at the Esprit de Corps Riding Academy. Here, you can learn to ride horses while enjoying true eco-tours. They offer small group and private horseback trail rides that include trotting and cantering in a lush forest reserve near Kapa'a. Even beginners can join in, as the academy provides beginner trail rides, ensuring everyone can enjoy the experience. Riding through the scenic landscapes on horseback offers a different perspective and a tranquil connection with nature.

At the Esprit de Corps Riding Academy, you can embark on a horseback riding adventure tailored to your skill level. Whether you are a seasoned rider or a beginner, the academy offers lessons and trail rides to suit your needs. Their eco-tours provide a unique opportunity to explore the lush forest reserves near Kapa'a. You can join small group rides or opt for a private session, enjoying the tranquility and beauty of the surroundings. Trotting and cantering through the trails, you will feel the rush of adventure and the peaceful connection to the natural environment.

Photo Opportunities in Kapa'a

Let's have a look at the photo opportunities in Kapa'a.

Ke Ala Hele Makalae (Kapa'a Coastal Path)

The 8-mile Ke Ala Hele Makalae coastal walking and biking path is a photographer's dream. It stretches along the coastline, providing endless opportunities to capture the stunning beaches, rolling waves, and vibrant sunrises or sunsets. As you walk or bike along the path, you will find numerous spots to take pictures of the pristine coastline and lush greenery that frames the path. The ever-changing light throughout the day offers a variety of moods and tones to your photographs.

Kapa'a Town

The heart of Kapa'a is its charming downtown area, filled with historic buildings, quaint shops, and inviting restaurants. The streets are alive with color and character, making it a perfect spot for capturing the essence of small-town life. The monthly art walk is particularly photogenic, as the streets fill with local artists displaying their works, live music, and vibrant crowds. The blend of old and new, traditional and modern, provides a rich tapestry for street photography.

Wailua River

Flowing through lush, verdant landscapes, the Wailua River is a serene location for nature and landscape photography. Whether you are capturing the reflections of the greenery in the calm waters, the wildlife along its banks, or the kayakers and paddleboarders enjoying the river, there are countless opportunities for stunning shots. Early morning mist and late afternoon light can add a magical quality to your photos.

Sleeping Giant Mountain

The iconic Sleeping Giant mountain formation is a dramatic backdrop for any photo taken in and around Kapa'a. Visible from many points in the town, this mountain offers a powerful presence in landscape photos. Hike the trail up to its summit for panoramic views of the island, providing breathtaking photo opportunities of the valleys and coastline below.

Beaches

Kapa'a Beach and Waipouli Beach are idyllic locations for capturing the beauty of Kauai's coastline. These beaches offer classic seascapes with their golden sands, azure waters, and swaying palm trees. Sunsets here are particularly spectacular, with the sky painted in hues of orange, pink, and purple. Photos of beach activities, such as surfers catching waves or families enjoying a picnic, add a dynamic element to your portfolio.

Coconut Marketplace

The Coconut Marketplace in Kapa'a is an open-air shopping complex that bursts with color and energy. It's a lively spot for lifestyle and portrait photography, with its vibrant stalls, local vendors, and cultural performances. The mix of bright tropical decor and the relaxed island vibe provides a fun and engaging setting for capturing the essence of Kauai's local life.

Each of these locations in Kapa'a offers unique photo opportunities, making it a paradise for photographers looking to capture the natural beauty and vibrant culture of Kauai. Whether you are a professional or an amateur, you will find plenty to inspire your lens.

Nearby Attractions

Here are some of the nearby attractions that you cannot miss.

Kauai Coast Path

The Kauai Coast Path stretches along the island's eastern shoreline, offering a picturesque route for outdoor enthusiasts. Whether you prefer cycling, jogging, or simply strolling, this 8-mile-long path provides stunning waterfront views that showcase the beauty of Kauai's coast. As you traverse the path, you will be treated to panoramic vistas of the Pacific Ocean, with the sound of crashing waves accompanying your journey.

Kapa'a Beach and Waipouli Beach

Just a stone's throw away from Kapa'a town, you will find the inviting shores of Kapa'a Beach and Waipouli Beach. These pristine stretches of sand offer the perfect setting for a day of beach activities or simply unwinding by the water's edge. Whether you are building sandcastles with the kids, taking a leisurely swim in the ocean, or basking in the warm Hawaiian sun, these beaches provide an idyllic escape from the hustle and bustle of everyday life.

Wailua River

The tranquil Wailua River, located near Kapa'a, beckons adventurers to explore its serene waters and lush surroundings. Kayaking along the river offers a unique perspective of Kauai's natural beauty, with opportunities to spot native wildlife and immerse yourself in the island's rich ecosystem. Boat tours are also available for those looking to relax and soak up the scenery while learning about the area's history and culture. Whether you are seeking adventure or simply seeking solace in nature, the Wailua River promises an unforgettable experience for visitors to Kapa'a.

Resorts in Kapa'a

Whether you are looking for luxury, family-friendly amenities or a budget-friendly stay, Kapa'a has something to offer. For a luxurious experience, Kauai Coast Resort at the Beachboy is a top choice. Nestled along the scenic Royal Coconut Coast, this resort features spacious suites, a beautiful pool area, and direct beach access. The on-site restaurant offers delicious local cuisine, and the tropical gardens provide a tranquil atmosphere perfect for relaxation.

Another great option is the Aston Islander on the Beach. This beachfront property combines comfort and convenience with its cozy rooms, ocean views, and laid-back island vibe. The location is ideal for exploring nearby attractions, and the poolside bar is a fantastic spot to unwind with a cocktail. For families, Plantation Hale Suites offers a welcoming environment with spacious condos equipped with kitchens, multiple pools, and barbecue areas. Its central location makes it easy to explore Kapa'a and beyond, providing a comfortable base for family adventures.

Budget travelers will appreciate the Kauai Shores Hotel. This affordable beachfront hotel offers colorful, modern rooms and a fun, relaxed atmosphere. With an on-site restaurant, complimentary breakfast, and evening entertainment, it is a great value for those looking to enjoy Kauai without breaking the bank. For a more intimate stay, consider the Hotel Coral Reef Resort. This boutique hotel features oceanfront rooms, a beautiful pool area, and personalized service. Its location near the Kapa'a bike path makes it perfect for those wanting to explore the area by bike or on foot.

Another fantastic choice is the Waipouli Beach Resort and Spa. This luxury resort offers beautifully appointed condos, a stunning pool with waterfalls and slides, and a beachfront location. The on-site spa provides a range of treatments, making it an ideal spot for relaxation. Lastly, the Courtyard by Marriott Kauai at Coconut Beach provides a blend of comfort and convenience with its modern amenities, beachfront access, and central location. The resort's pool, fitness center, and on-site dining options ensure a pleasant stay for all guests.

Kapa'a's diverse range of resorts ensures that every traveler can find the perfect place to stay while enjoying the natural beauty and vibrant culture of Kauai.

Chapter Fifteen

Toward the Summit of Mt. Wai'ale'ale

P lanning a day trip to the west side of Kauai? A journey toward the summit of Mt. Wai'ale'ale, one of the wettest spots on Earth, promises an unforgettable adventure. This chapter will guide you through the essentials, ensuring you make the most of your visit. The west side of Kauai offers a stark contrast to the more developed eastern and western parts of the island. Its rugged beauty, rich history, and secluded nature spots make it a must-see. As you venture toward Mt. Wai'ale'ale, you will encounter breathtaking vistas, lush valleys, and cascading waterfalls.

This trip is perfect for those who love the outdoors and want to experience the raw, untamed side of Hawaii. The west side is not just about the destination; the journey itself is filled with awe-inspiring landscapes. Whether you are driving through Waimea Canyon, known as the "Grand Canyon of the Pacific," or hiking along the scenic trails, every moment is a photo opportunity.

How to Reach the West Side of Kauai From Lihu'e Airport

Reaching the west side of Kauai from Lihu'e Airport is straightforward and offers several convenient options. Whether you prefer the freedom of driving yourself, the ease of a taxi, or the affordability of public transportation, you can find a suitable way to travel to the island's picturesque west side.

Car Rental

Renting a car at Lihu'e Airport is one of the most convenient ways to explore Kauai. Major car rental agencies like Hertz, Avis, and Enterprise have counters at the airport, making it easy to pick up a vehicle upon arrival. Once you have your car, you will take Ahukini Road from the airport. This road connects to various highways, including the main highway that runs across the island. From there, it is a scenic drive to the west side, where you can explore attractions like Waimea Canyon and Polihale State Park at your own pace. Having a car also gives you the flexibility to stop and enjoy the stunning viewpoints and local eateries along the way.

Taxi

For a more direct and personalized mode of transportation, taxis are readily available at Lihu'e Airport. A taxi ride offers the convenience of door-to-door service, taking you directly to your destination on the west side. This option is especially useful if you are traveling with a lot of luggage or prefer a more comfortable and private ride. The taxi drivers are usually knowledgeable about the island and can provide some local insights during your trip. Keep in mind that taxi fares can add up, especially for longer distances, but the convenience might be worth the cost.

Bus

The County of Kauai's Kaua'i Bus service is a dependable choice if you're looking for a cost-effective option. The bus system includes routes that connect the airport to various parts of the island, including the west side. Two bus routes stop at Lihu'e Airport daily, providing a cost-effective way to reach your destination. While taking the bus might take a bit longer due to multiple stops, it is an excellent way to experience local life and see more of the island from a different perspective. The buses are clean and well-maintained, and they offer a chance to relax without worrying about navigating the roads yourself.

Each transportation option has its benefits, depending on your preferences, budget, and travel style. Whether you choose the independence of a rental car, the comfort of a taxi, or the economy of the bus, you will be well on your way to exploring the beautiful and diverse landscapes of Kauai's west side.

Must-See Destinations

Exploring the west side of Kauai unveils a series of must-see destinations that capture the island's unique charm and natural beauty.

Hanapepe

Hanapepe, often referred to as "Kauai's Biggest Little Town," is a delightful destination brimming with character. This quaint town is a treasure trove of art galleries and historic buildings, each telling its own story of the island's past. Stroll down the main street, and you will discover a vibrant art scene with galleries showcasing local artists' works. The Hanapepe Swinging Bridge is a highlight, providing a fun and slightly adventurous experience as you walk across this historic suspension bridge. Friday Art Night is a local favorite, where the town comes alive with music, food, and an open-air art market. It is a perfect opportunity to mingle with locals, enjoy live entertainment, and savor delicious local cuisine.

Kauai Coffee Company

Eleele, the Kauai Coffee Company offers an immersive experience for coffee lovers and curious visitors alike. As the largest coffee grower in Hawaii, this plantation invites you to explore the fascinating world of coffee production. The guided tours walk you through the lush coffee fields, detailing the journey from bean to cup. You can also enjoy tastings of their various coffee blends, savoring the rich flavors that Kauai's unique climate produces. The visitor center provides an excellent opportunity to purchase freshly roasted coffee and other coffee-related products, making it a perfect stop for a souvenir that truly captures the essence of Kauai.

Barking Sands Beach

Barking Sands Beach, located on the west side of Kauai, offers a serene escape from the more crowded beaches. Its name comes from the unusual "barking" sound that the sand makes when walked on, a result of the specific shape and size of the sand grains. This beach is part of the larger Pacific Missile Range Facility, which means it is relatively secluded and less frequented by tourists. The expansive stretch of golden sand and the sound of the waves create a peaceful environment, perfect for a relaxing day by the ocean. It is an ideal spot for a quiet picnic, sunbathing, or simply soaking in the untouched beauty of Kauai's coastline.

Kalalau Lookout

Perched within Koke'e State Park, the Kalalau Lookout offers one of the most stunning vistas on Kauai. At an elevation of approximately 4,000 feet, this lookout provides panoramic views of the breathtaking Napali Coast, renowned for its rugged sea cliffs and verdant valleys. The lookout is easily accessible by car, with a short walk from the parking area to the viewing platform. On a clear day, the view extends far across the Pacific Ocean, while on mistier days, the valleys below take on an ethereal quality as the clouds drift through. It is a photographer's paradise and a place that truly embodies the dramatic beauty of Kauai's landscapes.

Waimea Canyon and Koke'e State Park

Waimea Canyon and Koke'e State Park are two of Kauai's most captivating natural attractions. Known as the "Grand Canyon of the Pacific," Waimea Canyon stretches approximately 14 miles long, over a mile wide, and plunges to depths of more than 3,600 feet. The dramatic collapse of the volcano that originally formed Kauai and the erosion of the Waimea River are what created this geological wonder. The result is a landscape of striking red and green layers, showcasing the island's volcanic origins and natural beauty.

Cultural Significance

The name "Waimea" translates to "reddish waters" in Hawaiian, a nod to the red soil erosion that colors the water during heavy rains. Beyond its geological significance, Waimea Canyon holds a rich cultural history. The area was once home to ancient Hawaiian settlements, and the land is imbued with stories and legends passed down through generations. Interpretive displays within the park offer valuable insights into this cultural heritage, helping visitors understand the deep connection between the land and its people.

Exploring Waimea Canyon

Waimea Canyon State Park offers a wealth of activities for nature enthusiasts and adventurers alike. Numerous hiking trails wind through the wilderness, providing access to some of the most scenic and remote areas of the canyon. Whether you are looking for a leisurely walk or a challenging trek, there's a trail to suit every level of experience. Popular hikes include the Canyon Trail to Waipo'o Falls, which offers stunning views and a rewarding waterfall at the end.

Scenic Drives and Vantage Points

For those who prefer a more relaxed exploration, the scenic drives through Waimea Canyon State Park are an excellent option. Several lookout points along the road provide breathtaking panoramas of the canyon's vast expanse. Key vantage points such as the Waimea Canyon Lookout and the Puu Hinahina Lookout offer unparalleled views of the canyon's deep gorges and vibrant colors, perfect for photography or simply soaking in the natural beauty.

Adventure Activities

For a more exhilarating experience, consider the Waimea Canyon downhill bike ride. This guided adventure takes you from the top of the canyon down to sea level, offering an exciting and unique way to see the landscape. Private tours are also available, providing personalized and in-depth exploration of the canyon's many features. Helicopter tours offer a bird's-eye view of Waimea Canyon and the neighboring Napali Coast, revealing the full grandeur of Kauai's rugged terrain.

Koke'e State Park

Adjacent to Waimea Canyon, Koke'e State Park extends the natural wonders with lush forests, additional hiking trails, and more stunning vistas. This park is known for its cooler climate, native vegetation, and abundant birdlife. Hiking trails in Koke'e range from easy walks to challenging treks, each offering a unique perspective on the island's diverse ecosystems. The Kalalau Lookout in Koke'e State Park provides one of the most spectacular views of the Napali Coast, making it a must-see for any visitor.

Waimea Canyon and Koke'e State Park together offer a comprehensive outdoor adventure that blends natural beauty, cultural history, and thrilling activities. Whether you are hiking through the canyon, enjoying a scenic drive, or taking in the views from above, these parks provide unforgettable experiences for everyone exploring Kauai.

Adventure Activities in Waimea and Koke'E State Park

Exploring Waimea Canyon and Koke'e State Park is an adventurer's dream come true. These parks offer a plethora of activities that cater to thrill-seekers, nature lovers, and anyone looking to immerse themselves in the stunning landscapes of Kauai. From the rugged terrain to the lush forests and breathtaking vistas, there's no shortage of excitement and beauty to be found here.

ATV Tours

For a heart-pounding adventure, hop on an ATV and navigate the rugged terrain of Kipu Ranch. ATV tours take you through breathtaking landscapes, lush forests, and sparkling waterfalls. It is a thrilling way to explore the natural beauty of the area while satisfying your need for speed and adventure.

Ziplining

Ziplining in Waimea is an unforgettable experience. Soar through the treetops and over valleys, getting a bird's-eye view of the stunning scenery below. Several companies offer zipline adventures that provide an adrenaline rush and a unique perspective of the area's lush landscapes.

Helicopter Tours

For a truly breathtaking adventure, take a helicopter tour over Waimea and the surrounding lands. These tours offer a once-in-a-lifetime opportunity to see the island from above, with aerial views of waterfalls, coastal cliffs, mountains, and the majestic Na Pali Coast. It is an experience that offers unparalleled views and memories that will last a lifetime.

Hiking

Exploring Waimea on foot is a must for any outdoor enthusiast. The Waimea Canyon offers a range of hiking trails, from easy walks to challenging hikes. These trails lead to lookout spots and scenic views that are simply spectacular. Koke'e State Park also boasts a variety of trails that cater to different skill levels, allowing you to explore lush rainforests, unique plant life, and stunning vistas. Whether you are an experienced hiker or just looking for a leisurely stroll, there's a trail for you.

Scenic Drives

If you prefer to explore from the comfort of your car, scenic drives through the parks offer panoramic views of Waimea Canyon and the surrounding landscapes. These drives provide a relaxing and picturesque way to experience the park's beauty, with plenty of opportunities to stop and take in the view.

Photography

Waimea Canyon and Koke'e State Park are a paradise for photography enthusiasts. The diverse landscapes, including the canyon's dramatic vistas and the lush forests, provide endless opportunities for capturing stunning images. Whether you are a professional photographer or just love snapping photos, you will find no shortage of inspiration here.

Birdwatching

Koke'e State Park is a haven for birdwatchers. The park is home to a variety of native bird species, including the endangered Hawaiian honeycreepers and the iconic 'I'iwi bird. Bring your binoculars and enjoy the chance to observe these beautiful creatures in their natural habitat.

Stargazing

Due to its remote location and dark skies, Koke'e State Park is an ideal spot for stargazing. As night falls, the sky comes alive with celestial wonders, offering a chance to marvel at the stars and observe the wonders of the night sky. It is a serene and awe-inspiring way to end a day of adventure.

Polihale State Park and Beach

Polihale State Park and Beach is a hidden gem on the westernmost tip of Kauai. Known for its expansive sandy beach and breathtaking views, Polihale offers a serene escape from the more crowded areas of the island. The majestic Napali

Coast, which borders the beach to the north, provides the ideal setting for a day of adventure and relaxation.

Directions

To reach Polihale, head west from Lihue on Highway 50 until you reach the small town of Waimea. From there, follow the signs to Polihale State Park. Be prepared for a bumpy ride—the final stretch of the journey involves driving on an unpaved dirt road that can be challenging, especially after rain. A four-wheel-drive vehicle is recommended.

Essential Tips

- Bring plenty of water and snacks, as there are no stores or restaurants nearby.

- The dirt road can be rough; drive slowly and cautiously.

- Check weather conditions before heading out; heavy rain can make the road impassable.

- Pack out all trash and belongings to keep the park clean and beautiful.

Amenities

- **Parking:** There is a spacious parking area near the beach.

- **Restrooms:** Basic restroom facilities are available.

- **Showers:** Outdoor showers are provided to rinse off sand and saltwater.

- **Picnic Areas:** There are designated picnic areas with tables for a scenic meal.

- **Grills and Pavilions:** Grills and shaded pavilions are available for public use.

Family Activities

Polihale is a great spot for family outings. The long stretch of beach is perfect for building sandcastles, playing beach games, or simply enjoying a leisurely walk along the shore. The gentle slope of the beach makes it ideal for wading and splashing in the shallow waters, though always keep an eye on the ocean conditions as the currents can be strong.

Beach Activities

- **Bodyboarding and Surfing:** The waves at Polihale can be great for bodyboarding and surfing, particularly for more experienced surfers.

- **Picnicking:** Set up a picnic at one of the tables or on a blanket in the sand, and enjoy the stunning surroundings.

- **Watch a Sunset:** Polihale is renowned for its spectacular sunsets. Stay until evening to witness the sky ablaze with colors.

- **Shore Fishing:** Anglers can try their luck fishing from the shore, with a chance to catch various local fish.

- **Spot the Dolphins and Whales:** Keep an eye out for dolphins playing in the surf or, during the winter months, humpback whales breaching offshore.

- **Boating:** Launch a boat from nearby and explore the waters around Polihale.

- **Snorkeling:** While the surf can be strong, on calm days, snorkeling can be enjoyable, revealing an array of marine life.

- **Swimming:** The waters can be inviting for swimming, but caution is advised due to potential strong currents.

- **Camping:** Polihale offers a remote camping experience. Obtain the necessary permits and enjoy a night under the stars.

- **Hiking:** Explore the trails and dunes surrounding the beach for a bit of adventure and exercise.

Accommodation on the West Side

Accommodation on the west side of Kaua'i may not be as abundant as on the North Shore, East Coast, and South Shore, but what it lacks in quantity, it makes up for in charm and proximity to nature. The West Side offers a handful of inns and plantation cottages nestled in the picturesque towns of Waimea and Hanapēpē, providing a cozy retreat with easy access to the island's stunning natural attractions like Waimea Canyon and Kōke'e State Park.

Waimea Plantation Cottages

For a quintessentially Hawaiian experience, Waimea Plantation Cottages offer a charming stay in historic, restored sugar plantation cottages. Each cottage is uniquely furnished, providing a rustic yet comfortable base to explore the wonders of the West Side. Guests can enjoy beachfront views, lush gardens, and a tranquil atmosphere that harks back to old Hawaii.

The West Inn Kauai

Located in the heart of Waimea, The West Inn Kauai is a great option for those seeking convenience and comfort. This modern inn offers well-appointed rooms and suites with all the amenities you need for a relaxing stay. Its central location means you are just minutes away from exploring Waimea Canyon, visiting local shops and restaurants, and enjoying the nearby beaches.

Hanapēpē Inn

For those looking to immerse themselves in the local arts scene, the Hanapēpē Inn is a delightful choice. Situated in the artistic hub of Hanapēpē, this charming inn offers cozy accommodations with easy access to art galleries, boutiques, and eateries. The inn's vintage decor and warm hospitality make it a perfect spot to unwind after a day of adventure.

Waimea Canyon Villas

For a more private and spacious stay, consider the Waimea Canyon Villas. These vacation rentals provide all the comforts of home, with fully equipped kitchens, multiple bedrooms, and living areas. Ideal for families or groups, the villas offer a serene retreat just a short drive from the breathtaking vistas of Waimea Canyon and the lush trails of Kōkeʻe State Park.

Camping at Keke State Park

For the truly adventurous, camping at Keke State Park is an unforgettable experience. The park offers several campgrounds where you can pitch a tent and sleep under the stars, surrounded by Kauaʻi's pristine natural beauty. It is a fantastic way to fully immerse yourself in the island's landscapes, with hiking trails and scenic viewpoints right at your doorstep.

While the West Side of Kauaʻi may not have the extensive accommodation options found in other parts of the island, the unique inns and cottages here offer a charming and convenient base for exploring the region's incredible natural wonders. Whether you are seeking a historic plantation cottage, a modern inn, or a rustic camping experience, the West Side has something to offer every traveler.

Popular Beaches on the West Side of Kauai

Exploring the west side of Kauai reveals some of the island's most beautiful and serene beaches, each offering unique experiences and breathtaking views. Here's a guide to the must-visit beaches on this stunning coastline.

Polihale State Park

Polihale Beach is renowned for its expansive stretch of golden sand and incredible sunset views. This remote beach offers a sense of seclusion and tranquility, making it perfect for those looking to escape the crowds. The drive to Polihale can be challenging due to unpaved roads, but the journey is well worth it for the breathtaking scenery and peaceful atmosphere.

Kekaha Beach

Kekaha Beach is known for its long, sandy shoreline and is one of the best spots on the island for sunbathing and beachcombing. The beach provides a picturesque setting for a relaxing day by the water. Strong currents can make swimming risky, so it is best suited for walking, picnicking, and enjoying the spectacular ocean views.

Salt Pond Beach Park

Located near Hanapepe, Salt Pond Beach Park is a family-friendly destination with calm waters protected by a natural reef. This beach is ideal for swimming, snorkeling, and exploring tide pools. Facilities such as picnic tables, restrooms, and showers make it a convenient spot for a full day of fun and relaxation.

Pakala Beach

Pakala Beach, also known as Infinities, is a favorite among surfers for its consistent waves. The beach itself is beautiful and less crowded than other spots, offering a serene environment. It is a great place to watch skilled surfers ride the waves or to try surfing yourself if you are experienced.

Barking Sands Beach

Part of the Pacific Missile Range Facility, Barking Sands Beach is not always accessible to the public, but when it is, it offers stunning, unspoiled views and a quiet retreat. The name comes from the sound the sand makes when walked on, adding a unique auditory experience to your visit.

In the next section, we will explore the southern shore of Kauai island.

Chapter Sixteen

All the Way to the South

The southern shore of Kauai is a treasure trove of beauty and adventure, perfect for planning an unforgettable trip. This region boasts sun-drenched beaches, charming towns, and lush gardens. Known for its sunny weather and stunning coastline, the South Shore is home to popular destinations like Poipu Beach, Spouting Horn, and the Allerton Garden. Whether you are looking to relax on the golden sands, snorkel in crystal-clear waters, or explore the rich cultural heritage, this area has something for everyone. From the quaint shops and eateries in Old Koloa Town to the breathtaking views along the Mahaulepu Heritage Trail, the South Shore offers a delightful mix of activities and sights. Dive into this guide to discover all the must-see spots and hidden gems that make the southern coast of Kauai a favorite among visitors.

How to Reach South Shore From Lihu'e Airport

Getting to the South Shore from Lihu'e Airport is straightforward, with several convenient transportation options available:

- **Car rental:** Renting a car from one of the major car rental agencies at

Lihu'e Airport is an efficient way to travel to the South Shore. You can easily access the main highways, such as Highway 50, which will take you south toward popular destinations like Poipu. This option offers the flexibility to explore the area at your own pace and visit various attractions along the way.

- **Taxi or rideshare:** Taxi and rideshare services like Uber and Lyft are readily available at Lihu'e Airport. These services provide direct transportation to the South Shore, offering a more personalized and comfortable ride if you prefer not to drive. Simply request a ride via your app, and you will be on your way.

- **Shuttle service:** Many hotels and resorts in Kauai offer shuttle services for their guests, which can be arranged in advance. Check with your accommodation to see if they provide shuttle services to the South Shore. This option can be convenient and hassle-free, especially if you are staying at a larger resort.

- Public transportation: The South Shore is connected to other areas of the island by the County of Kauai's Kaua'i Bus service. You can take a bus from Lihu'e Airport to reach your destination, although this option may involve transfers and longer travel times. The bus service is a cost-effective way to travel, but it is important to check the schedules and routes in advance to ensure a smooth trip.

Must-See Destinations on the South Shore

Shipwreck Beach is a top spot for adventurers and thrill-seekers. This beach, known for its impressive cliffs and rugged hiking terrain, exudes a laid-back Hawaiian energy. It is perfect for those looking to dive into some adventure. Whether you are cliff diving, hiking the coastal trails, or simply enjoying the dramatic ocean views, Shipwreck Beach is a must-visit for any adventure lover. Old Koloa Town offers a nostalgic glimpse into Hawaii's past. This historic community features century-old buildings, quaint gift shops, art galleries, and delightful dining options. Walking through Old Koloa Town feels like stepping back in time, providing a charming and immersive experience that highlights Hawaii's rich history.

Poipu Beach is a paradise for beach lovers. Renowned for its soft sands and excellent snorkeling opportunities, Poipu Beach invites visitors to relax and explore its vibrant marine life. The calm, clear waters make it an ideal spot for swimming and snorkeling, offering a serene setting for both relaxation and water activities. The Maha'ulepu Heritage Trail near Koloa is a must-see for nature enthusiasts and hikers. This scenic coastal trail offers stunning views of the coastline, showcasing the area's natural beauty. As you hike along the trail, you will encounter diverse landscapes, from rugged cliffs to serene beaches, making it a perfect spot for photography and nature appreciation.

Located in Lihue, the Kaua'i Museum is an essential stop for those interested in the island's history and culture. The museum showcases artifacts and exhibits that highlight Kauai's heritage, providing a deep dive into the island's past. From ancient Hawaiian artifacts to displays on the island's more recent history, the Kaua'i Museum offers valuable insights into the rich cultural tapestry of Kauai

Places to Stay on the South Shore

For a luxurious experience, the Grand Hyatt Kauai Resort & Spa is a top choice. This resort offers elegant rooms, beautiful gardens, and a lavish spa, perfect for relaxation. The resort's dining options and pools add to the overall indulgence, making it an ideal spot for those seeking high-end amenities. Kiahuna Plantation Resort Kauai by OUTRIGGER provides more laid-back, condo-style accommodation. With its beachfront location, lush gardens, and spacious units equipped with kitchens, it is great for families and those who prefer a home-away-from-home feel. The resort's proximity to Poipu Beach makes it a convenient and scenic place to stay.

Ko'a Kea Resort on Poipu Beach is perfect for couples or solo travelers looking for a boutique experience. This intimate resort offers oceanfront rooms, personalized service, and a serene atmosphere. It is an excellent choice for a romantic getaway or a peaceful retreat by the sea. Poipu Plantation Vacation Rentals offers charming cottages and vacation homes, providing a cozy and private stay. These rentals are ideal for travelers who want more space and the comforts of home. The location near Poipu Beach adds to the appeal, making it easy to explore the area. Poipu Kapili Resort offers luxury condo accommodations with ocean views and upscale amenities. This resort is perfect for those who want the convenience of a condo with the added benefits of a resort, such as a pool and tennis courts. It is a great option for travelers looking for a blend of comfort and sophistication on the South Shore.

Popular Restaurants on the South Shore

The South Shore of Kauai is a food lover's paradise with an array of popular restaurants. For fresh seafood and a lively atmosphere, make your way to the Beach House Restaurant. Its oceanfront location offers stunning sunset views, perfect for a romantic dinner. For a taste of local Hawaiian cuisine, Keoki's Paradise is a must-visit. The restaurant's tropical ambiance and menu featuring island favorites make it a hit with both locals and visitors. If you are in the mood for a gourmet burger or fresh fish tacos, head to Puka Dog. Known for its unique Hawaiian-style hot dogs, it is a fun spot for a quick and delicious meal. For breakfast or a casual brunch, Little Fish Coffee is a favorite. With its charming atmosphere and tasty acai bowls, it is the perfect way to start your day on the South Shore.

Popular Beaches on the South Side of Kauai

The South Side of Kauai boasts several stunning beaches, perfect for various activities and relaxation. Brennecke's Beach is a favorite for bodyboarding enthusiasts, thanks to its consistent waves and lively atmosphere. Kiahuna Beach, located near the Kiahuna Plantation Resort, offers soft sands and calm waters, ideal for swimming and sunbathing. This beach is perfect for families and those looking to unwind. Lawai Beach, known for its excellent snorkeling conditions, provides an underwater paradise for those looking to explore marine life. The clear waters and vibrant coral reefs make it a must-visit for snorkelers. For a more secluded and rugged beach experience, Mahaulepu Beach offers scenic beauty and tranquility. This beach is less crowded and provides a fantastic setting for hiking, beachcombing, and simply enjoying the natural surroundings.

Chapter Seventeen

Makamae Adventures (Precious, Valuable, Cherished)

This chapter is all about planning your visit to the unique attractions of Po'ipu, Koloa, Spouting Horn, and other nearby wonders. The South Shore offers a blend of natural beauty, historical charm, and thrilling activities that promise an unforgettable experience. Whether you are exploring the vibrant marine life at Po'ipu Beach, wandering through the historic streets of Old Koloa Town, or marveling at the natural geyser of Spouting Horn, these adventures capture the essence of Kauai's precious and valuable sites. Get ready to uncover the delights that make the South Shore a must-visit destination on your island itinerary.

Po'ipu Beach Park

Po'ipu Beach Park, located on the South Shore of Kauai, is a favorite spot known for its crystal-clear waters and family-friendly atmosphere. This crescent-shaped beach is equipped with amenities like parking, lifeguards, restrooms, showers, picnic tables, and a natural wading pool perfect for young swimmers. Visitors and locals enjoy a variety of activities here, including surfing, fishing, snorkeling, and bodyboarding. For those seeking adventure, there's a bodyboarding site suitable for older children and novice adults, a surfing area for experienced surfers, and a reef ideal for snorkeling. The beach is also known for occasional sightings of Hawaiian monk seals lounging on the shore. Additionally, during the winter months, from December through April, you might catch a glimpse of humpback whales in the distance. When visiting Po'ipu Beach Park, it is important to follow safety guidelines, respect marine life, and stay aware of ocean conditions to ensure a safe and enjoyable experience.

Spouting Horn

Spouting Horn is a fascinating blowhole located on the southern coast of Kauai in the Koloa district. This natural wonder is renowned for its dramatic display, where crashing waves erode lava rocks along the coastline, creating narrow openings. With each wave, water shoots upward through these openings, reaching heights of up to 50 feet. The resulting spray creates a distinctive hissing sound, which is tied to a local legend about a giant lizard that was once trapped in the blowhole. Visitors to Spouting Horn can marvel at this impressive display of nature and hear the eerie sound that recalls the trapped lizard each time the blowhole blasts water into the air. The site is a highlight of the Koloa Heritage Trail, a 10-mile trail that showcases the rich history and natural beauty of the region. Spouting Horn offers a distinctive and memorable experience, whether you are interested in local folklore or geological formations.

Allerton Garden

Allerton Garden, also known as Lāwaʻi-kai, is a stunning botanical garden on the south shore of Kauai, Hawaii. Designed by John Gregg and Robert Allerton, this 80-acre paradise is tucked away next to Lāwaʻi Bay in a valley formed by the Lāwaʻi Stream. As one of the five gardens of the non-profit National Tropical Botanical Garden, Allerton Garden is renowned for its meticulously crafted garden rooms, pools, miniature waterfalls, fountains, and statues. Visitors can explore the garden through guided tours, which offer an immersive experience of beautifully designed landscapes and captivating art exhibits. The garden's enchanting scenery has made it a popular filming location, featuring in movies and TV shows like South Pacific, Jurassic Park, and Pirates of the Caribbean. Whether you are a nature enthusiast or a film buff, Allerton Garden's picturesque setting and rich history provide a memorable visit.

Koloa Town

Koloa is an unincorporated community and census-designated place (CDP) in Kaua'i County, Hawai'i, United States. Known for its historical significance, Koloa was the site of the first successful sugarcane plantation in the Hawaiian Islands, established in 1835. Omao to the northwest and Poipu to the south border Koloa, which is on the southern side of Kauai. The town's rich history is deeply tied to the sugar industry, and it has managed to retain much of its old-world charm with old-fashioned storefronts and plantation buildings now housing shops and local businesses. Part of the larger Koloa district, the area extends from Old Koloa Town to the picturesque South Shore near Poipu, offering visitors a unique glimpse into Hawaii's past and cultural heritage. Whether you are strolling through the quaint streets, exploring historical sites, or simply enjoying the laid-back atmosphere, Koloa offers a blend of history and charm that captures the essence of old Hawaii.

Conclusion

Whether you are embarking on a solo journey of self-discovery, seeking a romantic escape with a loved one, or enjoying quality time with family and friends, Kauai offers an abundance of experiences to nourish the soul and rejuvenate the spirit. From the lush landscapes and pristine beaches to the vibrant culture and rich history, Kauai has a way of capturing the heart and leaving a lasting impression.

As your time on Kauai comes to an end, take with you the memories of its unparalleled beauty and the warmth of its people. The Garden Isle is not just a destination; it is a place that invites you to slow down, breathe deeply, and connect with the natural world in a profound way. The island's tranquility and splendor will remain with you long after you depart, gently calling you back to its shores time and time again

We hope this book has inspired you to explore all that Kauai has to offer and has provided you with the insights and information to make your journey unforgettable. As you reflect on your adventure, we invite you to share your experiences and leave a review. Your feedback helps us continue to provide valuable resources for future travelers, ensuring they, too, can experience the magic of Kauai. Mahalo and safe travels!

Mahalo

A s we close the final page of this book, I want to express my deepest gratitude for joining me on this remarkable journey through the heart and soul of this enchanting land with its rich tapestry of culture, breathtaking landscapes, and thrilling adventures. This is not just a destination—it's an experience that leaves an indelible mark on your soul.

If you've enjoyed the adventure, I'd love to hear about it. Your reviews and feedback are the lifeblood of authors, guiding future travelers on their own quests. So, take a moment to share your thoughts. Your words may inspire the next adventurer to explore with the same enthusiasm and wonder.

Your support and feedback mean everything as I continue on this journey of sharing the adventure magic with the world. Mahalo nui loa for your time and consideration.

With warmest aloha, Ocean Breeze Adventures

Keep an eye out for our next adventure, The Big Island!

Can't wait? Here is a chapter to help!

Chapter 6: The Hidden Gem of Hawaii

Welcome to the most volcanic place on Earth, home to the most active volcano in the world: Kilauea, which has been almost continuously erupting since it was first documented in 1983. If you want to see a volcano in action, the Big Island is where you need to be.

How to Get to Puna

Puna has the same transport options as the rest of the Big Island: you can rent a car, use the Hele-On Bus (the inter-island public bus that serves Hilo, Puna and Kona), take a taxi or shuttle, or take a tour bus. However, if you want to experience the remoteness and uniqueness of this diverse and rugged district on your own terms, with the freedom to stop and explore the natural wonders and unique character of the place as you wish, then renting a car is the best option. Once you are on the ground in Puna, the roads are challenging, with many built around lava flows and in poor condition. If you are unfamiliar with the island, drive cautiously, especially on the winding, one-lane roads. Keep out of restricted areas and respect private property signs.

About Puna

Geography and Climate

Puna encompasses just under 320,000 acres (500 sq. miles), a little smaller than the island of Kauai. The landscape has gentle slopes and no discernible watersheds. It receives a great deal of rain, particularly in the north and high elevations. Puna is dominated by the active volcanoes Mauna Loa and Kilauea. The district sits on the volcanic rift zone of Kilauea and has been subject to frequent lava eruptions and flows.

Vegetation ranges from thick rainforest to shrubs amid lava rock. Native forest areas of Kahauala and Wao Kele o Puna are home to unique species such as the endangered Hawaiian honeycreeper birds, which include the 'apapane and 'i'iwi, known for their vibrant red plumage. You might also encounter the rare Hawaiian fern, or 'ama'u, and the endemic 'ōhi'a lehua tree, which bursts with striking red blossoms.

History

A sacred island since early times, Puna is known for its emphasis on Hawaiian spirituality and mythology, with Pele, the goddess of fire and volcanoes, said to live in the district. For many centuries, people valued Puna for its lush rainforests, fertile land and abundant natural resources, providing cultural and economic sustenance for generations. Native Hawaiians dance the hula, chant oli, and weave lauhala in Puna, and plantations produce sugar, macadamia nuts, and other food crops.

The district is known for its black sand beaches (the prettiest is Kehena Black Sand Beach, where spinner dolphins like to hang out) and, as far as anyone knows, it's the only place on the Big Island where you can see live lava flowing. Puna's relatively inaccessible location and lava have also attracted a population of eccentrics: 'hippies, funky artists, alternative healers, Hawaiian sovereignty activists, pokalolo [marijuana] growers, organic farmers and off-the-grid survivalists all call this unique region home.

Near Pahoa, the Kapoho tide pools are filled with tropical fish, sea turtles, and octopuses, making them a snorkeler's paradise. Ahalanui Beach Park features a large, spring-fed thermal pool that offers a unique and relaxing swimming experience. The warm waters of the pool are heated by geothermal activity, providing a natural spa-like setting amidst the lush surroundings.

Must-See Destinations

Lava Tree State Monument

This park features the remnants of a wet 'Ōhi'a forest that was overrun by a historic lava flow from an eruption in 1790. This lava flow is significant because it preserved the shapes of the trees in lava molds, creating an intriguing and unique landscape that offers a glimpse into the island's volcanic activity and the resilience of its natural environment. A simple, winding trail runs through the park, and there are several gazebos along the way for picnicking.

Kapoho Tide Pools

Lava rock pools rimmed with tropical fish, sea turtles and octopuses are popular with snorkelers (some of the tide pools left at Pahoa were destroyed in the 2018 Kilauea eruption).

Kehena, Black Sand Beach

This local nudist beach has black-sand and frequented by spinner dolphins. It's a great place to spend the day.

Kalapana

Now a national monument, the area was a bustling community before being completely covered by the 1990 lava flow from Kilauea. Today, you can hike to ruins of the town and to the 'new' black sand beach that's formed.

Volcano National Park

Although not technically in Puna, this national park is just a 30-minute drive and features the Kilauea Caldera and Thurston Lava Tube.

Places to Eat

There are some very good fine dining and casual places to eat in Puna, including local food. You can get a gourmet meal at Paolo's Bistro in Phoa, excellent local dishes at Kaleo's Bar & Grill, or casual eats at places like Pahoa Fresh Fish and Boogie Woogie Pizza.

Places to Stay

Bed and Breakfasts

For something smaller and more intimate, there are plenty of BnBs, including Lava Tree Tropic Inn and Aloha Junction Bed and Breakfast.

Vacation Rentals

Options for vacation rentals include VRBO and Airbnb, which offer more room and amenities better suited to groups or families, from beach cottages to rainforest retreats.

KAUAI TRAVEL AND ADVENTURE GUIDE COPY

Camping

Some of the more adventurous among you might want to camp out at one of the many parks and campsites in and around Puna; there are plenty of options, so do check with the individual parks and campsites for regulations and permits. Here are two camping options to consider:

Namakanipaio Campground: Located within Hawaii Volcanoes National Park, Namakanipaio offers a unique camping experience surrounded by lush rainforest. The campground provides tent sites, rustic cabins, and amenities such as restrooms and picnic tables. It's an ideal spot for those wanting to explore the park's volcanic landscapes and hiking trails. Remember to secure a permit in advance and be prepared for cooler temperatures at this higher elevation.

Kalopa State Recreation Area: Situated just north of Puna, Kalopa State Recreation Area features a serene setting with a native forest backdrop. This campground offers tent sites, cabins, and access to hiking trails that wind through the lush forest. Facilities include restrooms, picnic areas, and outdoor showers. It's a great option for those looking to immerse themselves in nature while being a short drive from the attractions in Puna. As with all state parks, check the regulations and obtain any necessary permits before your visit.

Boutique Hotels

For discerning travelers, there are some boutique hotels that offer all the luxury and service of a grand hotel but with the personal attention of a small inn. One great example is the Kilauea Lodge, a rustic boutique hotel which was actually built on the site of the original 1938 YMCA camp for workers on the volcano. The Kilauea Lodge Restaurant, which serves meals made with local produce and island flavors, is located right on-site, with its dining room and adjoining outdoor lanai (veranda) overlooking the gardens.

Luxury Resorts

For those seeking a few more creature comforts, hotels like the Volcano House offer luxurious amenities, beautiful vistas, and impeccable service to guests. Volcano House is perched on the rim of the Kilauea caldera in Hawaii Volcanoes National Park and it offers guests a unique lodging option. Established in 1846, the historic hotel sits at the front door of one of the most active volcanoes on Earth. Guests have a view into the volcanic landscapes and geothermal activity unlike anywhere else.

At Volcano House, 33 guest rooms in the lodge and 10 cabins throughout the park offer varied options to suit a range of visitors' needs and budgets. The guest rooms in the lodge are spacious and meticulously designed to showcase the beauty of Hawaii Volcanoes National Park. Guests who prefer a more rustic experience can choose a cabin located deep within the park, offering them a more natural setting while providing basic amenities.

Dining is an event in itself at Volcano House, with the main restaurant, The Rim, occupying the entire top level of the hotel. Floor-to-ceiling windows offer unobstructed views of the Kilauea caldera, with the main dining area overlooking the lava lake. Open for breakfast, lunch, and dinner, the menu features imaginative takes on local Hawaiian cuisine using locally sourced and seasonal ingredients.

It's easy to get to the Thurston Lava Tube, Devastation Trail, and Jaggar Museum from the hotel, or walk to the visitor center, which has exhibits and information about Kilauea's history and current activity. Staying at Volcano House completely immerses you in the volcanic environment of this Big Island icon and offers a unique and deeply memorable stay. Whether you get to witness the luminous glow of the lava at night or wander through the lush rainforest during the day, Volcano House is certain to leave a lasting impression on anyone who stays.

Exploring Further

This chapter has taken you to one of Hawaii's best-kept secrets, the district of Puna. If you are looking for wonderfully unique scenery, exciting attractions, cultural and historical experiences, or just sheer beauty, Puna is your Big Island spot. If you've taken a 10-day trip to the Big Island, you've probably spent at least one day of it in Puna, whether you knew it or not. It's that easy to find. If you've been to the Big Island and didn't make it to Puna, then you've missed out on one of the most unique regions of Hawaii. The next chapter will take you into the great outdoors of Puna and describe the various activities you can do there. It's going to take you into the deep end of Puna!

If you would like to get an advanced copy before it goes live, go to oceanbreezea dventures.net

I can also be reached at

Email: diana@oceanbreezeadventures.net

Instagram: @freel.publishing.llc

Facebook: Freel Publishing LLC

TikTok: @freel.publishing

See you there!

About Ocean Breeze Adventures

D iana Freel is an avid adventurer and best-selling author of her Travel and
Adventure Guides. Her journey began on the sandy shores of Oahu,
where the ocean's whisper ignited her wanderlust. When her 50th birthday cruise
was cancelled, she went on a mission to learn everything about Oahu, especially
her love for adventurous excursions. She then realized not everyone has the drive
and resources to do all that research and felt compelled to share her knowledge
with others who love sand, sun, and palm trees. Ocean Breeze Adventures was
born. Her Travel and Adventure Guides can be found on Amazon. You can
follow her on social media (@FreelPublishing) and her website, www.oceanbr
eezeadventures.net

Follow Diana and her amazing travel guides. Want to see where she goes next? Can't wait for the next travel guide? She publishes her Aloha Weekly Newsletter every Friday. Scan the QR code to sign up.

Happy Adventures, Diana Freel, owner of Freel Publishing and Ocean Breeze Adventures.

Also by Me

Ocean Breeze Adventures

- Oahu Travel and Adventure Guidehttps://www.amazon.com/dp/B0CX9MVSXV

- Oahu Young Adventurers Companion Activity Bookhttps://www.amazon.com/dp/B0D12K1TP3

- Maui Travel and Adventure Guidehttps://www.amazon.com/dp/B0CZNGXC55

- Kauai Travel and Adventure Guidehttps://www.amazon.com/dp/B0DC4KR92Y

- Audio Books – Found on Audible

  - Oahu Travel Guide

  - Maui Travel Guide

- Coming soon

  - The Hawaiian Islands Cruising and Adventure Guide

  - Alaska Cruising and Adventure Guide

  - Costa Rica Travel and Adventure Guide

Freel Publishing

- The Dad Joke Training Guide: For New and Expectant Fathers https://www.amazon.com/dp/B0D58TMB81

- Space Coloring Book for Kids: 4–8 https://www.amazon.com/dp/B0D12K3W3P

- Diabetes Logbook for Type 1,2, and Gestational Diabeteshttps://www.amazon.com/dp/B0D12TX6ZB

- Travel Journal: Chronical Your Journey Around the World

- NICU Journal: Chronicling Your Journey Through the Neonatal Intensive Care Unit

- Notebook: College Lined

- Chic Gardens: Greening Your Urban Space https://www.amazon.com/dp/B0DBGP4MY3

Diana Freel

- Your First Saltwater Aquarium

  - Coming soon

    - The Last Snapshot: A Willow Creek Mystery Novella

- Frosting and Foul Play: A Willow Creek Mystery

Chapter Eighteen

Sample Itineraries

One Week Adventures

Day 1: Arrival and Relaxation

- Arrive on Kauai and get settled into your accommodations.

- Spend the afternoon unwinding on one of Kauai's stunning beaches, like Po'ipu Beach or Hanalei Bay.

- Enjoy dinner at a local restaurant, savoring fresh seafood and traditional Hawaiian cuisine.

Day 2: North Shore Exploration

- Head to the North Shore and visit iconic spots like the Napali Coast, Hanalei Bay, and Princeville.

- Take a scenic hike along the Kalalau Trail or visit the picturesque Hanalei

Pier.

- Have dinner at a farm-to-table restaurant in Hanalei, enjoying locally sourced dishes.

Day 3: Outdoor Adventures

- Embark on an adventure like kayaking on the Wailua River or hiking to Wailua Falls.

- Visit cultural sites like the Wailua River State Park or the Fern Grotto.

- Relax in the evening with a traditional Hawaiian luau, complete with music, dance, and delicious food.

Day 4: East Side Exploration

- Explore the charming town of Kapa'a and visit attractions like Lydgate Beach Park and the Kauai Museum.

- Enjoy outdoor activities such as snorkeling at Kealia Beach or hiking the Sleeping Giant Trail.

- Sample local cuisine at a food truck or cafe in Kapa'a, indulging in flavorful Hawaiian dishes and refreshing tropical drinks.

Day 5: South Shore Relaxation

- Spend the day on the South Shore's beautiful beaches, like Po'ipu Beach or Lawai Beach.

- Take a leisurely stroll along the Maha'ulepu Heritage Trail or enjoy a scenic drive along the coast.

- Treat yourself to a rejuvenating spa treatment or massage, followed by a romantic dinner at a seaside restaurant.

Day 6: West Side Adventure

- Explore the rugged landscapes of the West Side, visiting Waimea Canyon and Polihale State Park.

- Take a scenic drive along Waimea Canyon Drive, stopping at viewpoints to admire the vistas.

- Enjoy a sunset picnic at Polihale Beach, watching the sunset over the horizon.

Day 7: Departure

- Take one last stroll along the beach or explore any remaining sights or activities.

- Pack up and check out of your accommodations, reflecting on the week-long adventure.

- Depart from Kauai with a heart full of aloha and a promise to return.

Family-Friendly Vacation

Day 1: Arrival and Beach Day

- Arrive on Kauai and get settled into your family-friendly accommodations.

- Spend the day playing on one of Kauai's family-friendly beaches, like Lydgate Beach Park or Po'ipu Beach.

- Enjoy a casual dinner at a beachfront restaurant, watching the sunset as you dine.

Day 2: North Shore Fun

- Head to the North Shore and explore family-friendly spots like Hanalei Bay and the Hanalei Pier.

- Take a family hike along the Hanalei River or visit the Kauai Mini Golf and Botanical Gardens.

- Enjoy dinner at a family-friendly restaurant in Hanalei, with dishes that kids and adults will love.

Day 3: Outdoor Adventures

- Embark on a family-friendly adventure like kayaking on the Wailua River or hiking to Wailua Falls.

- Visit cultural sites like the Kamokila Hawaiian Village or the Kauai Children's Discovery Museum.

- Treat the family to a traditional Hawaiian luau with entertainment and activities for all ages.

Day 4: East Side Exploration

- Explore Kapa'a and visit family-friendly attractions like Lydgate Beach

Park and the Ke Ala Hele Makalae coastal path.

- Enjoy activities like biking or snorkeling at Kealia Beach.

- Sample local treats at a shave ice stand or bakery in Kapa'a, indulging in sweet and refreshing snacks.

Day 5: South Shore Relaxation

- Spend the day on the South Shore's family-friendly beaches, like Po'ipu Beach or Baby Beach.

- Take a family snorkeling adventure at Lawai Beach or go on a boat tour to see marine life.

- Enjoy a family dinner at a casual restaurant, sharing stories of the day over delicious Hawaiian fare.

Day 6: West Side Adventure

- Explore the natural wonders of the West Side, visiting Waimea Canyon and Koke'e State Park.

- Take a scenic drive along Waimea Canyon Drive, stopping at viewpoints for family photos.

- Enjoy an evening barbecue at your accommodations, grilling local favorites, and dining under the stars.

Day 7: Departure

- Take one last family stroll along the beach or a morning swim before checking out.

- Pack up and bid farewell to Kauai, promising to return for more family adventures.

- Depart from Kauai with cherished memories and happy hearts.

Made in the USA
Columbia, SC
18 December 2024